Healing the Shattered Soul

Becoming the Person God Intended

James L. Hanley
C. Tracy Kayser

James L. Hanley & C. Tracy Kayser

Moriah

Freedom Ministries

Table of Contents

James L. Hanley & C. Tracy Kayser

Table of Figures

James L. Hanley & C. Tracy Kayser

Preface: Beginning the Journey

Since the early 1990s, I have been involved in praying for the inner healing and deliverance of Christians suffering from a wide array of symptoms—symptoms they believed to be spiritual attacks.

This path—like so many others I have ventured down in my life—was not one I set out to take. It began fairly early in my ministry. I was serving as an associate pastor responsible for Christian education and counseling when two women came to me for guidance. One had satanic ritual in her background, and the other, though not as entrenched in the occult, came from a family that explored many different "spiritual disciplines." Though their backgrounds were unique, both women were steeped in occult exploration and one had even experienced ritual abuse. They came to me separately, on different days, but I recall the events as one story.

Both women were experiencing demonic visions and terrifying nightmares. Both were hearing voices and holding conversations with spiritual entities. My first inclination was to refer them to a counselor outside the church, but they begged me to help them get deliverance. Both women knew the entities that were tormenting them. One knew the entity as a familiar spirit that she had invited into her life many years before—something that her family had encouraged. The other woman's spiritual tormentor came to her when she was being assaulted as a child. Every time she was abused she would hear its voice and sense its mocking presence. By the time she came to see me in her adulthood she had left behind a trail of counselors who just wanted to *talk about* her experience. She was adamant that she needed deliverance, which is why she came to me, a Christian minister, and not to yet another counselor.

I had witnessed both of these ladies in their Christian walk and their sincere commitment impressed me. So I was somewhat astonished that they could not shake their demonic symptoms since my background and formal training had taught me that a "Christian could not be demon-possessed." I had no doubt that these women were born-again believers, so I marveled that they were experiencing symptoms that closely resembled demon-possession.

I tried the usual remedies. "Let's read the Scriptures that proclaim our freedom. We can rebuke the evil spirits, resist them, and they must flee." This approach was neither encouraging nor liberating. With one of the ladies we even tried a prayer team approach with laying on of hands, anointing with oil, and fervent prayer. All to no avail. At a pastor's prayer meeting the following week, however, I brought up my experience with the two ladies for collective prayer. We included them in our petitions to the Lord.

Two pastors approached me afterward with some suggestions. First, they shared that they too had experienced some of the same issues in counseling. The first pastor asked if I had heard of Dr. Neil T. Anderson's *Freedom in Christ Ministries*, based in La Mirada, California, and suggested that I contact him. The other pastor suggested that I speak to Dr. Charles Kraft, a professor at Fuller Seminary in Pasadena. I called both ministries that very day.

Charles Kraft responded first and sent a young man named Greg Knopf who was in his Master Level class on Spiritual Warfare and a member of one of his prayer teams. My first impression was that Greg was something of an intern in one of Kraft's classes, but soon learned that he was very highly skilled, scripturally knowledgeable, and a delight to work with in ministry. Greg explained to me that it was possible for a Christian to have demonic spirits. Although he used the term "demonization" and not "demon-possession," he began answering my many questions. Once I was assured that this was not some sort of deviant spiritual practice, Greg asked me to invite the ladies to come in so he could try to help set them free. One was reluctant at that time, but the other quickly volunteered.

That turned out to be my first deliverance experience. Though I was only an observer during the process, I was so intimately involved that I could not deny what I had seen and experienced. Based on that experience, however, I could not simply jettison all my prior notions and understanding (from teaching and the Scriptures) about demon-possession. Instead, the experience drove me back to the Scriptures. I began building an extensive library of spiritual warfare materials, which continued to grow over the years. During the following two months I devoted myself to studying all the biblical passages I could unearth to affirm or deny the doctrine of demon-possession and the Christian. As I studied the relevant passages in context, my doctrine on demonization began to shift. In a later chapter I will detail my discoveries and why I now believe based on the Scriptures that a Christian can in fact have a demon.

After hearing the testimony of the first lady's deliverance, the second lady also came in for prayer. Before long, word spread about the freedom these women experienced after Greg and I prayed with them, and others began seeking help and deliverance. Greg let me observe him as he ministered to one after another who came seeking freedom. One young lady from our congregation came in to see me, and as I began to schedule an appointment with Greg she said "No!" She did not know nor trust Greg. She wanted me—and me alone—to help her. Like a deer caught in the headlights I was stunned. I caught my breath and tried to remember everything I had seen and learned from Greg. Then I stepped out. God honored me that day, and I realized that God could use me just as He used Greg.

From that day many years ago to this very day I have been praying and counseling with people who just seem to appear out of the woodwork. They come through referrals from individuals who have experienced newfound freedom and from various ministries that have partnered with us.

I believe that God has been training me in a unique way. For a season He sent me *easy* cases, from which I was able to learn about power encounters through demon confrontation. Though that concept may sound very intimidating it really wasn't. Through Greg's mentoring I learned that I could forbid the enemy to manifest in unwanted ways using an ordinary voice. God had me do this for the first few years and then He began to teach me a different approach. Instead of working with spirit after spirit I found that I could simply use Neil Anderson's spiritual survey material to clean out the majority of issues and then go after the enemy to remove what was left over.

Over the years God has taught me by sending waves of people with similar spiritual issues. At first I dealt with those who required testing of "counterfeit spiritual gifting." Then I worked with individuals

9

diagnosed with Multiple Personality Disorder (MPD), currently called Dissociative Identity Disorder (DID). Last year, God led to me a stream of people suffering from same-sex attraction. (My co-author Tracy will share her testimony because she struggled in that area.) Currently God is sending me a wave of people with "flipsides," which I will explain in a later chapter. I am a slow learner, but I trust that He will help me figure out what He is trying to teach me now. In the meantime He always seems to fill in the gaps where I am lacking.

To date I have had the opportunity to pray in over 5,000 sessions (typically lasting an hour and a half) and worked with 3,000–4,000 different clients. The experience has been invaluable. My objective in this book is to share some of the lessons I have learned with you. We also invite those of you who have refined certain areas where we may be lacking to contact us so that we can enjoy and apply your discoveries in our own ministry.

As I share my own journey, I recognize that many ministries have been on parallel paths since the early 1990s. From my discussions with others who minister in spiritual warfare I have recognized that God uses all of us—some with similar approaches to the ministry and others with dramatically different approaches. I offer my own approach and experiences not as the *final word* or *only way* that God works but rather to share how He has led me in my own ministry. God allows us to use various different means and methods in our ministries and blesses many approaches to set the captives free. The fundamental principle that unites us all is this: *following Jesus as He leads*.

One final note: The names of all individuals in the following pages (with the exception of my co-author Tracy) are fictitious so as to protect the interests of the parties involved. Most case studies represent a specific individual while a few are composites that combine elements of many I have ministered to over the years.

Introduction: The Wounded Soul

Meet Ann. She represents many Christians I have counseled over the past few years. When I asked her why she wanted to see me, Ann rattled off a laundry list of symptoms. First and foremost was her *sensation of demonization*—meaning that she felt demonic oppression. Ann reported intermittent feelings of rage followed by episodes of fear and panic. Like many whom I have ministered to over the years Ann had been in traditional counseling and, based on her symptoms, was diagnosed as manic depressive or suffering from Bipolar Disorder. As we talked Ann shared that she felt various inner conflicts. She said that she loved her parents but sometimes hated them. Likewise, her faith in God was solid and yet sometimes she felt alienated from Him and then experienced guilt and shame.

Ann's spiritual journey included many years of counseling as well as attempts to secure her freedom through deliverance ministries. During those sessions she had experienced temporary relief on occasion but complete freedom eluded her. As a result she felt further disappointment with God, and had even begun questioning her faith.

Ann's condition is puzzling because in most other respects she presents as a spiritually strong, mature Christian. She understands many aspects of spiritual warfare and is far more knowledgeable than most of her fellow believers, in part owing to her own spiritual journey. Though she has collected a library of books on deliverance and spiritual subjects, she admits that she has great difficulty reading them.

Ann attends church regularly and participates actively in a small group. She admits that church attendance is extremely difficult and that she always arrives late to any function. Although she volunteers for ministry and has been faithful for a number of years, she admits that everything is an internal struggle. Beneath a highly-functioning façade Ann struggles with depression, sadness, and anxiety.

In reviewing her childhood Ann shares many difficulties with her parents. She was hurt deeply when her mother and father divorced when Ann was seven years old. She had to grow up quickly and feels that her childhood was stolen. To make matters worse her father neglected his responsibility of paying child support, which left Ann feeling further unloved and unvalued.

What Is This?

My experience has taught me that when someone shares a testimony like Ann's standard deliverance approaches are usually ineffective until the person achieves inner healing. I assign the person a preliminary diagnosis of dissociation ("fortresses" or "strongholds" in biblical terminology), and then proceed to test the diagnosis. The testing is fairly simple even for lay counselors, but it does require the understanding and participation of the person seeking help.

Two problems

There are two problems that must be resolved in helping Ann find complete healing and freedom. She definitely has spirits but they are more entrenched than the typical legal rights and strongholds we encounter in traditional spiritual warfare. Ann also has deep wounds from her childhood experiences that allow a separate territory where the enemy can find a perch. We call these fortresses. (2 Cor 10:3-5) In the following pages we will discuss the process of freeing someone who is experiencing demonization and also the process of deep level healing that is necessary for the cases like Ann's where fortresses are involved.

Part I: Understanding Spiritual Warfare

In Part I we will present a primer on spiritual warfare for deliverance ministry....

James L. Hanley & C. Tracy Kayser

Chapter 1: Theology of Satan and Demons

The Reality of Demons

One of the more effective schemes Satan's has used throughout human history is dividing humankind into one of two extreme camps. In the first camp are all those who have been led to believe either that Satan does not exist but is merely a figment of wild imagination or that, if he does exist, he is powerless against an invulnerable Christian.

In the second camp are all those who are preoccupied—even obsessed—with the devil and his power. In their zeal and excitement they spot demons lurking behind every bush. Eventually they render incredible what should basically be a credible belief. Both extremes are very dangerous and weaken the body of Christ. Christ came to set us "free." This includes setting us free from the clutches of spiritual powers, freedom from the clutches of sin, freedom from the clutches of this world, and freedom from the clutches of our fleshly nature.

I recommend many of the excellent, thorough scriptural studies on demonization such as C. Fred Dickason's *Demon Possession and the Christian,* Dr. Ed Murphy's *Handbook of Spiritual Warfare,* and Dr. Joe Albright's *Liberating the Bruised.* My intent here is not to retrace these authors' footsteps. Instead this section will provide you with a brief survey of the demonic condition, emphasizing things you will encounter in ministry. Quite often when we encounter someone who has heard a short refutation of "demon-possession and the Christian" all we really need to do to progress beyond the doubts and skepticism is quickly remove the stumbling blocks. As a Biblicist, I believe the Bible is inerrant and without contradiction. When a theological question seems to reveal an apparent contradiction, my initial response is to dive back into the Bible. Dr. Walter Martin used to say that 90% of apparent discrepancies are resolved by turning to the Scripture. Dr. David Regan once said in a sermon that any "text taken out of context is pretext."

After presenting a short introduction on demonology in the Old and New Testaments we will examine how demons penetrate our lives, survey major demonic symptoms, explore the question of Christian demonization, and finally address the 10 most common scriptural myths.

Evil Spirits and the Old Testament

The Old Testament simply assumes the existence of evil spirits and of Satan, the archenemy of God. God is pictured as surrounded by a heavenly host of spirits who do His bidding (Psalm 82:1; 89:6; Daniel 7:9-10). Beginning at the creation of the world and of man Satan worked through the serpent to cause man to fall into the grip of sin. The fall of man laid the basic foundation for God's entire redemptive plan, culminating in Jesus Christ's dying to triumph over Satan and draw man back into relationship with God.

Throughout the Old Testament evil spirits are always seen as being subject to the Father God. Satan appears with the "sons of God" to accuse Job and requests permission to put Job to the test. It is interesting to note that God initiated the discussion about Job and established all the parameters in which Satan could work. For instance, Satan was not permitted to take Job's life. A covenant existed between God and Satan. Although Satan was allowed certain powers and rights he was bound to obey the rules of God. This is in fact where we Christians find our power against him. Satan *must* follow our instructions when we take authority under the "law" of God.

Satan is found behind the idolatry of the nations (Psalm 106:36-37; 109:6). He is also behind David's sin of numbering the children of Israel (1 Chronicles 21). In order to end the plague that resulted from this sin, the angel of the Lord commanded David to offer a sacrifice upon the threshing floor of Onan. This site later became the location of the tabernacle and temple of the Lord. Satan can also be seen operating behind the powers of the king of Babylon (Isaiah 14) and the king of Tyre (Ezekiel 28). The prophet Zechariah portrayed Satan as a personage that the angel of the Lord opposed.

Demons and the New Testament

Every New Testament author mentions the existence of a literal devil, or Satan. Nineteen books mention him by name and eight mention the existence of demons or evil angels. The New Testament contains more than 250 references to evil spirits or demons. The Gospels refer to Satan 29 times, and in 25 of those Jesus is speaking about him as a personal being.

Throughout history some have argued that Jesus merely "played along" with the common beliefs of the Jewish people of His day and pretended that demons existed. Accordingly they contend that all the symptoms Christ healed were forms of sickness and insanity. This is erroneous, however, because the New Testament writers clearly distinguished demonism from other types of diseases. So they report that Jesus both healed the sick and cast out demons (Mark 1:32). Demonism was distinguished from both epilepsy (Matthew 4:24) and leprosy (Matthew 10:8).

In Jesus' day exorcism was a crude practice often intertwined with magic. While exorcists of the day used long, involved procedures which dated back to the wisdom of Solomon, Jesus could command demons out with a word. Observers would exclaim, "What is this? A new teaching with authority! He commands even the unclean spirits, and they obey Him" (Mark 1:27). The Jewish historian Josephus hailed Solomon as the most effective minister in deliverance.

The demonic theme was deeply entwined in the whole of Christ's ministry of redeeming man back to Himself—of the grip of sin and out of the grip of Satan. Jesus' death was to redeem man from bondage to the satanic kingdom and bring him into the kingdom of God. In fact, when Jesus came to proclaim the Gospel, He could not preach the Gospel we preach because He had not yet died and resurrected. Jesus' Gospel proclaimed that that the kingdom was coming and included casting out demons and healing the sick.

> "Jesus was going through all the cities and villages, teaching in their synagogues and proclaiming the gospel

of the kingdom, and healing every kind of disease and every kind of sickness. The news about Him spread throughout all Syria; and they brought to Him all who were ill, those suffering with various diseases and pains, demoniacs, epileptics, paralytics; and He healed them." (Matthew 4:23-24).

Let's look at some passages referring to Christ's ministry: "He went into their synagogues through all Galilee, preaching and casting out the demons" (Mark 1:39). He "cast out many demons and He was not permitting the demons to speak, because they knew who He was" (Mark 1:34). "And whenever the unclean spirits beheld Him, they would fall down before Him and cry out, saying, 'You are the Son of God!'" (Mark 3:11).

Later on in His ministry Jesus sent out the 70 to go and heal the sick and cast out demons. "And the seventy returned with joy, saying, 'Lord, even the demons are subject to us in Your name'"(Luke 10:17). After Jesus' death, resurrection, and ascension Peter described the Lord's ministry: "You know of Jesus of Nazareth, how God anointed Him with the Holy Spirit and with power, and how He went about doing good, and healing all who were oppressed by the devil; for God was with Him" (Acts 10:38).

We are at War

In both the Old and New Testaments we see that the real battle we wage is in the spiritual realm. Whereas the Old Testament introduces concepts, in the New Testament Jesus confronts the enemy directly. In the New Testament we learn where Jesus wants us to focus our attention.

> "For our struggle is not against flesh and blood, but against the rulers, against the powers, against the world forces of this darkness, against the spiritual forces of wickedness in the heavenly places." (Ephesians 6:12)

At the most basic level our battle is the truth against the lie. Jesus is the truth and Satan is the father of lies. Lies bind us mentally, emotionally, and even physically. The application of truth unbinds us and sets us free. Truth is the only remedy. This confrontation begins in the opening pages of Genesis when Adam and

Eve were seduced by the lies and continues until finally the "Truth" in the person of Jesus Christ sets us free.

Meanwhile in this age we are at war. The Apostle Paul wrote "in order that no advantage be taken of us by Satan for we are not ignorant of his schemes" (2 Corinthians 2:11). The responsibility of every Christian is to not be ignorant of satanic schemes and to be trained, at the very least, to recognize the enemy and to know when he or she is under spiritual attack. Some in our churches have yet to understand that we have a spiritual enemy and that apart from the grace of almighty God we are sitting ducks for Satan's target practice.

We Have Authority and Power

Soon after I began to walk in spiritual warfare I realized that my prayers were ineffective. It took several months for me to finally get the concept. Initially I would pray to God in the name of Jesus and ask Him to bind the enemy, send angels, or answer my petitions. One day I realized that it does *not* work that way. As I thought about the armor of God (Ephesians 6) it dawned on me that *I* was to be the warrior! That very day a huge transformation materialized in my thinking. I saw myself on the battlefield, and *I*—not God—was the soldier.... What an amazing shift! I was equipped with all the battle equipment I needed— the sword, the shield, and all the armor and protective gear. Furthermore, Jesus had already disarmed the enemy at the cross and promised in Romans to put "Satan under my feet" (Romans 16:20). In this imagery God is the general. He is not merely a soldier on the front line and He will not do the battle. Engaging the enemy in battle is my job.

In this imagery I saw my position as a player on the field with God as the head coach. Recasting the mental imagery from the battlefield to an athletic field helped me to understand the dynamics. Thus, if I find that Satan is defeating me; I know that it is because I have not engaged the enemy directly. Merely praying for God, the coach, to come out onto the field and run my plays for me will not do. It is against the rules! Just as policemen administer the will of the government established through its laws, so we are to administer the will of God established through His grace concerning our freedom.

What's more, we have been given authority over demons (Mark 3:14-15). Christians debate precisely what authority we believers have because of a passage in the book of Jude that records an unusual caution that states that the archangel Michael *dared not pronounce a judgment against the devil*. The question is whether can we take a position of authority vis-à-vis Satan when Michael, the highest angel in Heaven, seems, at best, to have limited authority.

> "But Michael the archangel, when he disputed with the devil and argued about the body of Moses, did not dare pronounce against him a railing judgment, but said, 'The Lord rebuke you!'" (Jude 1: 9)

The answer to the question is that we believers do, in fact, have more authority than angels and even archangels. Angels were not given authority over Satan; we were. We are the spiritual policemen. We are not bigger or better than Satan and his forces, but in the "rules" of Heaven we have been granted authority over them. Like the policeman who stands in an intersection, we can raise our hand and stop traffic. The enemy—just like the motorists—stop not because we are bigger or more powerful but because we are operating under authority granted to us. When we exercise our authority as God's spiritual policemen the enemy *must* obey our authority as long as we follow the rules. Furthermore once God, the Father, has given His authority He does not take it back. That means we not only have authority, but we also have the responsibility.

Returning to the warfare analogy, we are called to be soldiers stationed behind enemy lines seeking to save those who are lost by sharing the good news of the Gospel. When we find prisoners our duty is to release them from the shackles of bondage to the enemy. We are to be neither ignorant nor cowardly in our warfare but to stand firm on the Rock (Matthew 16:18), clothed in the armor (Ephesians 6:11-19), standing ready as we await the coming of our Lord Jesus Christ.

A More Powerful Encounter

After learning more and more of God's truth about how to deal with these forces, I have discovered that the truth itself is our power in defeating the evil one. Jesus said, "If you abide in my word, then you are truly disciples of Mine; and you shall know the truth, and the truth shall make you free" (John 8:31-32). I have not moved away from "power encounters" (a technique that involves addressing the enemy directly) but rather have found that placing the emphasis on truth results in a more powerful encounter. Dr. Neil Anderson would call this emphasis a "truth encounter." The more truth that we bring to the situation before us, the more power we have in delivering freedom—for it is "the truth that sets us free." But *having* truth is not enough; we must *apply* truth to each situation and circumstance with faith and boldness.

In addition to understanding dissociation (or fortresses), which we will examine in detail in Parts II and III, it is also imperative for us to have a clear understanding of the role of demons. Healing on both fronts—fortresses and demons—is required for a Christian to come totally free. I come from a very fundamental theological base and can certainly identify with the doubts that many experience when faced with demonic spirits, especially when it comes to demonic activity and oppression of believers. I had been taught that a Christian could not be demon-possessed. The hyphenated word itself—"demon-possessed"—was an anathema to my theological understanding of a Christian's position.

The following chapters are addressed to those who have reservations about demonic activity in the life of Christians. If you believe that Christians can be demonized, it might be enough for you to scan the chapters before proceeding just to ensure that we have a common understanding. Spend some time on the 10 myths to ensure that you can help clients who hold some of the most common misconceptions. You will discover many in the Church oppose these understandings. I have found that solid theological discussion—not emotions, personal opinions, or testimonies—is the way to address and overcome differences in theological understanding.

Chapter 2: Enemy Attack

"Be of sober spirit, be on the alert. Your adversary, the devil, prowls about like a roaring lion, seeking someone to devour. But resist him, firm in your faith, knowing that the same experiences of suffering are being accomplished by your brethren who are in the world." (1 Peter 5:8-9)

We must address several crucial questions when preparing to defend against the enemy: *How does Satan devour us? What are his weapons? What are his schemes? How are we to resist him?*

In considering this Scripture note that the symptoms appear as standard sufferings and experiences of mankind. Satan masks his attacks behind the common. Many of Job's experiences were common illnesses and afflictions that seemed "natural" or what we might term "bad luck."

Consider the kinds of manifestations that Jesus encountered when dealing with demonic spirits.

"And when Jesus saw that a crowd was rapidly gathering, He rebuked the unclean spirit, saying to it, 'You deaf and dumb spirit, I command you, come out of him and do not enter him again.'" (Mark 9:25)

How did Jesus know that this boy had an unclean spirit? The symptoms were exactly the same as those manifest in a person who was deaf and mute. Apparently Jesus had the gift of "discerning of spirits." The remarkable point is that this child had a demon *and* was physically infirm. Notice how the demonic spirit had hidden his presence behind (and within) a real illness.

"Demonization is not limited to extreme or bizarre behavior. Because we believed the myth that demonic influence is only evident in extreme or violent behavior and gross sin, we are unaware of much of Satan's activities or intrusions in the lives of 'normal' believers. Spiritual conflicts are much more common than we have believed. Most Christians who suffer from demonic influence lead relatively normal lives while experiencing many personal and interpersonal problems. These problem-plagued people wonder what's wrong with them and why they can't just 'do better.' It is not the raving demoniacs that are hindering the effectiveness of the church, but rather Satan's subtle deception and influence in the normal, churchgoing believers."[1]

Not all issues are demonic. Many of us tend to see a demon "behind every bush." This is simply not the case. We must take care not to become too focused on demons. Our focus must be on Christ at all times, but it would be a travesty to ignore such a simple spiritual release for someone who might be suffering demonization rather than a true physical affliction. A simple principle that I practice is: "When in doubt cast it out."

The Mind

Satan's first line of attack is the mind. To operate at maximum efficiency, the first lie he peddles is that he does not exist. Sometimes a variation occurs in which he tries to convince us that he is only found on the "mission" field. A third variation is that Satan can only attack non-Christians. If a person believes these lies it opens the door for an onslaught of undefended thought-abuses and truth-distortions.

Because Satan and his demonic forces are spiritual beings they could be whispering in our ears this very minute without our being aware of their presence. Recall how Peter, unaware that Satan was using him, rebuked Jesus concerning his death and resurrection. Jesus recognized that it was Satan and responded by rebuking the devil instantly, and then he rebuked Peter for not capturing his thoughts.

> "But He turned and said to Peter, 'Get behind Me, Satan! You are a stumbling block to Me; for you are not setting your mind on God's interests, but man's.'"
> (Matthew 16:23)

Paul warns us in 2 Corinthians 10:4-5 to "take every thought captive to make it obedient to Christ." *Satan's most devastating lies are those that destroy our ability to be disciples and to make disciples.* He attacks our identity in Christ with lies designed to induce us to believe that we are "worthless," "nothing," a "failure," and a "fool." To undermine our trust in God he points out all the evil in the world and gets us to blame God. Instead of telling us these things in the third person, demons get us to express them in the first person: "I am worthless," "I am nothing," or "I am a failure." The most freeing experience I had came the day I learned that I did not have to own every thought that came into my head.

Remember that Satan is a spirit being Satan that does not appear to us in the flesh. The accounts suggesting that he is able to manifest in human form seem to be illusions or hallucinations rather than true material bodily manifestations.

Shelley came to me several years ago reporting that her marriage and family life were in shambles. Her husband would yell at her and tell her that *she* was the problem in the marriage. Her children always blamed her—for anything and everything. She was defeated and beaten with words and thoughts. Her mind was consumed with thoughts that she was the problem. "I'm guilty," she would hear. "I'm stupid." "Everyone would be better off without me." The constant barrage of depressing and accusing thoughts had brought her to the brink of suicide.

In our first counseling session we spent over two hours discussing various issues in her life. The most important principle that Shelley took home that day was that these internal tapes were not her own. Many times we have reflected on the "truth" that began to set Shelley free—the truth that *she did not have to own everything she thought.*

Scripture commands us to capture thoughts (2 Corinthians 10:4-5). This means that we must examine every thought that pops into our minds. If the thought is not "truth in love" we must reject it. Rejection can be as simple as saying "I choose not to believe that thought." Realizing that her inner thoughts were not necessarily her own gave Shelley hope and strength. She was **not** the horrible, worthless person that she constantly played out in her head but rather a child of God, worthy, acceptable, and cleansed.

The next step with Shelley was to capture the thoughts her family members had spoken to her. Just as Satan used Peter against Jesus, Shelley's family was listening to and repeating Satan's accusations. They, too, needed to capture their thoughts, however initially they were not equipped. But Shelley, like Jesus, could examine everything that came to her from her husband and children and measure it against the standard: "truth in love."

We have counseled many individuals in our referral prayer ministry who believe they are hearing and speaking directly from God. They will carry on conversations with the Holy Spirit, Jesus, or God. The problem is that they are being deceived. The voices they hear are demonic spirits masquerading as one of the Persons of the Trinity. The test given in 1 John 4: 1-3 usually clears up the deception:[2] *The enemy will not be able to confess that "Jesus came in the flesh."*

The enemy uses various deceptions, such as convincing people that they are hearing from aliens who are emitting signals from UFOs or that the FBI is on their trail, bugging their homes or that they must live life on the run, hiding from the Mafia. The enemy uses such deceptions to assault people so strongly that no amount of reasoning or counter-argument will be able to dissuade them. We typically avoid direct confrontation of deceptions such as these and take the person through the *Steps to Victory*. The best approach in such cases is to let the Holy Spirit convict and retrain over a period of time. The key is to shut down the voices so that the truth can begin to penetrate.

A few months ago I was praying with a lady in her late 30s who had accepted Christ about five years earlier. She was having a very difficult time in her walk and listed "voices" among her symptoms. She had heard "voices" all of her life. After becoming a Christian she never thought to mention the condition to anyone because it had always been her experience and she assumed that all people heard voices. Sometimes the voices would try to guide her and at other times they would be give her suicidal directions. After several weeks of prayer and counseling she discovered that these voices could be expelled.

The Body

Have you ever had a headache but, instead of reaching for the aspirin bottle, you tried rebuking it? In cases when spiritual circumstances are surrounding some of the common distractions of life (such as a headache) I have found that making a spiritual command can bring significant release and relief. It is certainly worth the effort. On a few occasions I have had success in issuing simple commands to prevent dyslexia, stuttering, and indeterminate pains.

> "And behold, a man from the multitude shouted out, saying, 'Teacher, I beg You to look at my son, for he is my only boy, and behold, a spirit seizes him, and he suddenly screams, and it throws him into a convulsion with foaming at the mouth, and as it mauls him, it scarcely leaves him.'" (Luke 9:38-39)

Today we might diagnose this boy's illness as an epileptic seizure. The spirit was hiding his presence behind a physical malady. Scripture distinguishes between healing and demonic deliverance, and it also recognizes that some physical illnesses are demonically induced.

> "And the news about Him went out into all Syria; and they brought to Him all who were ill, taken with various diseases and pains, demoniacs, epileptics, paralytics; and He healed them." (Matthew 4:24)

Migraine headaches are one of the more common ailments I encounter. Often in the middle of a prayer session someone will share experiencing a sudden headache. We rebuke it, and in a matter of minutes the symptom fades away.

On several occasions I have found that the symptoms of epilepsy in both children and adults were of demonic origin. Merely praying, taking spiritual authority, and removing legal rights allow us to break the stronghold of epilepsy.

A fellow named Joseph was referred to us from Freedom in Christ Ministry. He had many issues that were disturbing him. Before we began to pray Joseph confided that he had dyslexia and would be unable to read. He had suffered with this affliction since high school and it was so severe that he was unable to finish his schooling. The *Steps to Victory* (moriahfreedomministry.com) require extensive reading, so I knew that we were in for a long and tedious session if we had to read each phrase aloud and have Joseph repeat it from memory. Just on an off chance I thought to make a command: "I forbid Dyslexia in Jesus' name." The enemy had affected his eyesight for 20 years, but after that rebuke Joseph was able to read the *Steps* with no problems.

A few months later another referral named Terry presented with a stuttering problem. I followed the same procedure—"I forbid stuttering in the name of Jesus"—and it ceased. Terry was able to read fluently without any sign of stuttering.

Though in some cases these maladies are physical, medical conditions, they can also be spiritual. I am very careful to explain to those I work with that not every physical condition is demonic. In many cases, however, demonic spirits can get away with causing physical affliction for years, or a even whole lifetime, if no one acknowledges that the condition might be spiritual—or at least have spiritual element. It is sad that so many individuals live bound when they could be free of serious oppression with a simple command. People who have experienced this instant freedom have felt as though Satan had cheated them out of life. That is *exactly* what he wants to do—"steal, kill and destroy"![3]

The Emotions

> "Be angry, and yet do not sin; do not let the sun go down on your anger, and do not give the devil an opportunity." (Ephesians 4:26-27)

Many veterans (of Vietnam and other police actions) have been referred to this ministry. During the process of confession many reveal a military circumstance that caused them to either take life or attempt to take life in a fit of rage. Long periods of fearful torment followed these aggressive acts. I recall a veteran who would huddle in the corner of his room screaming out in terror even though he was perfectly safe.

I have seen this same process play out in other situations involving demonic attachments. Take, for example, a man who is involved in sexual sin. In the process a succubus or incubus spirit could find a foothold. As the enemy gains strength in the man's life the sexual sin magnifies until, at last, the man becomes sexually obsessed and so consumed with it that he can think of practically nothing else.

Demonic attachment causes a person to experience the demons' emotions, which are exaggerated. My co-author Tracy, for instance, experienced bouts of rage, depression, jealousy, and loneliness that were exaggerated way out of proportion to the circumstance. Under the influence of a demon a situation that should evoke only a mild response can result in an overblown eruption of emotion.

After I bind the enemy it becomes apparent that the person was not experiencing his own emotions. They were totally of demonic origin, and thus when I bind the demon the person's emotions return to the normal range.

Similarly, a person may be harboring hurt or grief over some event that occurred in his/her life—perhaps the loss of a loved one. Feeling grief for a season over a loss is natural, but if the hurt and grief are masking an associated issue of unforgiveness against God there is a problem. In some cases a person will blame God for the loss of a loved one or some tragedy. This unforgiveness will give the enemy an opportunity to gain a foothold on the sadness. That spirit can then take the person deep into depression way beyond the natural experience of hurt and grief.

Apply this same concept to cases of fear, panic, eating disorders, and alcohol or drug abuse. When the enemy seizes the opportunity, all these symptoms become greatly magnified and exaggerated with destructive, life-crippling effects.

Chapter 3: Discerning Demonic Symptoms

Having expounded on the methods of demonic attack, it is indispensable to have a clear conception of how these manifest in particular symptoms. Let us start with the Lukan passage of the head demon Legion.

> "And when He had come out onto the land, He was met by a certain man from the city who was possessed with demons; and who had not put on any clothing for a long time, and was not living in a house, but in the tombs. And seeing Jesus, he cried out and fell before Him, and said in a loud voice, 'What do I have to do with You, Jesus, Son of the Most High God? I beg You, do not torment me.' For He had been commanding the unclean spirit to come out of the man. For it had seized him many times; and he was bound with chains and shackles and kept under guard; and yet he would burst his fetters and be driven by the demons into the desert. And Jesus asked him, 'What is your name?' And he said, 'Legion'; for many demons had entered him. And they were entreating Him not to command them to depart into the abyss." (Luke 8:27-31)

This is arguably the most severe case of demonization recorded in the Bible. I have met several individuals with symptoms very similar to this man's. In fact, I believe that many of the homeless people in our cities are in this condition. Notice that this man is not evil toward others but only toward himself. He is *self*-destructive. The modern media almost invariably portrays demonized people as dangerous to others, but in my own experience is that demonized people are dangerous to themselves.

Without Clothing

What we notice first about this man is that he was without clothing. It is very common to encounter demonized people who believe they must either wear or remove certain articles of clothing because spirits have convinced them that they must do it for salvation, to demonstrate obedience, or for some other false reason (the demons may have created a false doctrine). These people might be so confused that they simply cannot collect their thoughts long enough to put on clothes.

I first met Jerry in the office of an associate pastor of a local church. Jerry's behavior around the church had caused some school attendants to summon the police. He had apparently been yelling and gesturing in an aggressive manner and was not properly attired. The associate pastor, Bill, was able to pacify the authorities, who were not particularly interested in getting involved.

Bill invited Jerry into his office and called me. Fortunately, I was able to respond immediately. Bill knew that Jerry was having spiritual battles because he had come forward during church services seeking prayer and spiritual help. Jerry shared that he was hearing "voices" and had a sheaf of important papers that had been recorded by automatic writing (which we will discuss further in the next section).

When I walked into Bill's office, I noted that Jerry who was wearing a T-shirt and jeans was shoeless and wore only one sock. He was so preoccupied with his oppression that he did not realize that he was not fully attired. After Jerry experienced inner healing and deliverance, we were able to see him achieve spiritual victory and settle down on the road to freedom...*fully attired*.

On other occasions, I have seen spirits manifest and begin to strip clothing from a person in the midst of a prayer session. A quick command will halt the behavior.

Occult Powers

The second thing we note about the demoniac of the Gerasenes is his ability to discern the identity of Jesus (Luke 8:27-31). Demons know Jesus because He created them and they were in Heaven with Him before they fell. These demons knew exactly who Jesus Christ was— God incarnate—even though the disciples did not yet understand. Unfortunately they often see the spiritual enemy as well.

Many people I have prayed with have occult powers and receive demonic spiritual insight. Fortune-tellers, psychics, palm readers, and other occult channelers will speak of current or past lives and relate valid information. Demons have existed throughout time and relay information to occultists. Although on many occasions these spirits will give some accurate information, these powers are not trustworthy because they originate in lying, deceiving spirits.

> "It happened that as we were going to the place of prayer, a slave-girl having a spirit of divination met us, who was bringing her masters much profit by fortune-telling. Following after Paul and us, she kept crying out, saying, 'These men are bond-servants of the Most High God, who are proclaiming to you the way of salvation.' She continued doing this for many days. But Paul was greatly annoyed, and turned and said to the spirit, 'I command you in the name of Jesus Christ to come out of her!' And it came out at that very moment." (Acts 16:16-18)

When Christians come under the influence of this type of occult power it brings great bondage into their lives. In *The Bondage Breaker*, Dr. Neil Anderson speaks of a young man named Alvin who was noted for his prophecies and speaking in tongues. Although Alvin was ministering in many churches, his own life was disintegrating. When he first met Alvin, Dr. Anderson discerned immediately that Alvin's gifting was not from the Lord. Dr. Anderson then described how Alvin, who had been operating in occult power, was released from bondage.

Not long ago a troubled young married woman named Cindy was referred to our ministry. Cindy was having a difficult time walking away from her past occult lifestyle. As a child she had been spiritually sensitive, and her parents had encouraged her to develop "her powers."

31

As Cindy matured friends and family members sought her out more and more to give them "readings," and all agreed that she was supernaturally gifted.

Cindy accepted Christ, but as she began to mature in the Lord she found that she could not get away from her occult abilities and felt tormented by her "gifting." Cindy could sense what other people were thinking and she was powerless to stop. It had become such a natural part of her life that she thought it was normal.

As she continued using her powers Cindy noted that troubling experiences began to increase. Cindy would find herself angry with no justifiable cause and act out aggression both emotionally and physically. She would experience intense rage with a friend or family member without understanding why. She would beat her bed in rage for no apparent reason.

When Cindy was with her friends, she would sense (falsely) their evil and mocking thoughts about her. She could find no true inner peace and she could not shut off the occult input that was saturating her mind. Cindy did not experience freedom until she was finally convinced that this power was the doorway to demonic spirits and the primary cause of her oppression. Her freedom came when she was delivered from the spirits and her false gifting.

In the previous section I introduced you to Jerry, the shoeless young man. When Jerry first noticed my prayer partner, Anna, he looked very embarrassed and said, "Oh, you can see." Anna was gifted with "discerning of spirits," and she knew that Jerry was demonized. He then turned to me with a look of relief and said, "Thank God, you know what to do." Jerry had occult powers to know spiritual information about Anna and me. The truth was that I did not know what to do, but I knew some principles that would allow the Lord to minister through me.

Later, Jerry showed us some papers that he had brought with him. A spirit had written these letters and notes through automatic writing, and Jerry believed them to be messages from God and thus very important. Many of the writings were true scriptural statements whereas others were false prophecies. Like Cindy, Jerry had demonic spiritual revelations. After he confessed the sin of automatic writing and renounced the source of the revelations, they ceased.

It Seized Him

The enemy can affect a person for short periods of time with convulsions and other activities that mimic seizures or mental disorders or simply cause the person to run away.

My second deliverance prayer session was rather intimidating. It involved a young lady named Barb who had a history of seizures. I was surprised when, a few minutes into the session, she closed her eyes and tilted over in a deep sleep. Her behavior did not follow the patterns I had experienced with epilepsy. Suspecting a spiritual source, I began to issue commandments forbidding the enemy to manifest or cause seizures and to release her. Within a few minutes she became alert and was ready to continue our session. I later learned that she had been diagnosed with epilepsy, but in her case the enemy was trying to emulate seizures. To my knowledge she remains free from seizures to this day.

Based on this experience, I open all counseling sessions with a prayer that includes a command such as, "I forbid any manifestations, in Jesus' name." This simple command seems to be sufficient to prevent seizures and many other demonic distractions.

Another phenomenon that I notice from the pulpit is that the moment I begin talking about spiritual warfare, half the congregation begins to yawn and nod off. Now I recognize that my sermons are long and boring, but this malaise that I detect is so obviously spiritual that I have begun to stop and issue a few spiritual commands. Everyone then sits up and comes to attention.

On several occasions I have come into the counseling room and found the person I'm working with huddled in a corner, trembling. This occurs most often following a session with that person in which I have been commanding the enemy and casting out some spirits. The spirits know what might occur and are fearful. Sometimes the demons try to escape by causing the person to bolt. With no explanation the person will jump up and run out of the run. A simple command to the spirit, such as "I command you to bring _____ back in the name of Jesus and to sit down," is typically all it takes to shut down this behavior and induce the person to return.

Fear

In Luke 8:28 we read that the demoniac was terrified that Jesus was going to torment him. Some demons cause extreme fear. Recall the case of Saul in the Old Testament and how the spirits would incapacitate him with terror.

> "And it came to pass, when the evil spirit from God was upon Saul, that David took a harp, and played with his hand: so Saul was refreshed, and was well, and the evil spirit departed from him." (1 Samuel 16:23)

Leanne had low-grade anxiety that would cause her to be "on guard" most of her adult life. It would come on her with such force when she was driving that she would have to pull over on the side of the freeway and wait for the waves of terror to subside. A few hours of inner healing and evicting the enemy of fear proved to be life-changing for Leanne.

They Hate Worship and God's Word

In the passage from 1 Samuel we also see the effect of David's worship in releasing Saul from the torment. Saul knew that worshipping was the temporary solution for his terror.

I recommend worship music to everyone I work with to help to keep the enemy at bay.

Ellen accepted Jesus as her savior in jail. After she was released, the first time she went to church the enemy began threatening her and cursing her when she tried to enter the sanctuary. The voices in her head seemed to be audibly screaming and yelling at her. That first day she got stuck in the foyer in a state of fear, unable to enter the sanctuary where worship had already begun. The ministering chaplain who had led Ellen to Christ brought her to see me and we were able to release her from the spiritual tormenters.

Today Ellen is married and directs a halfway house for women where she helps those who suffer similar bondages.

He Burst the Fetters

Can demons impart strength? The demoniac of the Gerasenes was unusually strong. His strength may have been an outflow of demonic power or merely a byproduct of lacking the sensation of pain and physical awareness.

Phil exhibited unusual strength. He had been using various street drugs during the previous week and I was walking him through the *Steps to Freedom*. Many counselors acknowledge only the physical aspects of substance abuse and neglect the fact that there is also a spiritual empowerment.

As we were taking him through the material Phil suddenly began to speak with a mocking tone. This grew more intense by the moment, and then he bolted. Phil's brother Ray, who was attending the prayer session with him, feared he was heading for the knife drawer in the kitchen and managed to tackle him. But even though Ray was much larger Phil easily threw him aside. Another of Phil's friends was present, a karate instructor well over six feet tall. He proved no match for Phil, either, and was manhandled just as Ray had been. I was stunned at what was happening. As my wits came back I uttered a command, "Down, in Jesus' name." Immediately Phil was thrown to the floor as though a mighty invisible wrestler had just given him a spiritual body slam. There he lay for 10–15 minutes, unable to move, until he was back to his own senses. Like the demoniac of the Gerasenes, Phil had incredible power.

Another example of spiritual strength came from a young man who called for help. He asked if our prayer team could come to his house because he feared that the enemy would overpower him and cause him to lose control his driving. When he showed us into his house it was immediately obvious that his fears were justified, for nearly every wall and door in his home was pocked with fist-holes he had punched in anger. It was a miracle that he had not broken any bones. He was so focused—so mindless of the pain or consequences—that he was capable of doing incredible damage.

Although this young man could have posed a risk of physical danger to our prayer and counseling team, we were never concerned that any harm would come to us as we helped him. Simple commands "in Jesus' name" were sufficient to restrain his aggressive acts.

They Speak Through People

Demons can sometimes control people enough to speak audibly through them. This is rather common once the enemy realizes he has been exposed. More frequently, though, a person will begin to hear voices in his mind. This is especially the case with those who have been ritualistically abused or have used substances such as PCP, cocaine, or other mind-altering drugs. I have also observed strong demonic voice control among individuals who have been involved in occult practices such as fortune-telling, readings, channeling, and the like.

The enemy's power is limited, however, and the person is usually back in control within a few minutes. Whenever I suspect that a spirit is speaking through someone I stop the manifestation with a simple command such as "in the name of Jesus, I forbid the enemy to speak." Then I address the person and tell him to take control and engage his will because I do not want to empower the demonic spirits.

When a demonic spirit speaks through a person it uses the person's physical body and vocal chords. The person's tonal range immediately changes—sometimes rising higher and sometimes falling lower—and the pattern of speech will vary. Every person has a speech pattern that is distinct and natural for him or her. When a demonic spirit assumes control, you will note a sudden change in this natural pattern. In some cases, the person will speak with an accent or in a different, foreign language. In many prayer sessions I have heard old English as well as Spanish and French accents surface. In many cases the person will let fly a barrage of curse words and vulgar language in a prideful or mocking manner. The person's eyes will seem to have no real point of focus, and the countenance of the face will change. At times the voice will take on a more childlike or adult characteristic.

In the case of "legion" (in whom thousands of spirits were present) only one spirit controlled the conversation,[4] but it is possible for different voices to come from the same person. One man requesting our assistance would carry on a conversation with himself—a lower-pitched voice would exchange words with a higher-pitched voice. It was an amazing scene to watch and hear. If I had closed my eyes I would never have imagined that such distinct voices were coming from the same person.

While all of these manifestations are interesting to observe, allowing them to continue seems to empower the demonic spirits. Intervene to shut down these manifestations as quickly as possible to prevent empowering the spirits further. It is critical to help people regain and retain their own will and personality.

Hostile and Defiling Behavior

Sometimes a demonized person will exhibit extremely fierce or hostile behavior (Matthew 8:28-32; Acts 19:13-16). On many occasions demonic spirits speaking through people have threatened me or members of my family. When this occurs I cut off that assignment and forbid the enemy to carry out any of his threats. The enemy quite naturally wants to intimidate those of us in deliverance ministries, but I take heart in the fact that God is the one who "gives and takes life" (Deuteronomy 33:39-40).

Spirits are often called "unclean" because they cause the victim to behave in a manner that is defiling (Luke 4:33-36; Mark 1:25-26). So do not be surprised when demonized people curse and exhibit crude behavior and embarrassing mannerisms.

Cutting on Oneself

Cutting is a common demonic manifestation. The main spirit behind this behavior is Baal. The spirit causes a person to hurt until he or she makes an incision, at which point the pain is released. People who cut typically feel unclean or dirty and often suffer from eating disorders such as anorexia or bulimia.

Deborah was skinny as a rail when I first met her. She had all the classic symptoms of a Baal spirit— cutting, anorexia, and purging. As we worked with Deborah we found a young sub-part (sub-personality; we will examine dissociation and sub-personalities in Part II, "Understanding Fortresses") that thought she was evil and we suspected this was the demon. After several hours of inner healing and deliverance, we decided to take a break. Deborah went to the restroom adjacent to our counseling room to freshen up. As she entered the room and turned on the light she shrieked in horror. Deborah had just seen herself in the mirror as we all saw her—extremely thin—and had no idea that she was skinny. She had always seen herself as overweight.

Suicide Attempts

Demonic spirits are always trying to take our lives. But because they are spiritual beings and unable to do it themselves, they must deceive us into suicide attempts or other self-destructive behavior. We are not told how Satan intended to get Job to "curse God and die," but in Jesus' case he tried to trick the Lord into jumping off a cliff.

As Jeffrey was on his way to our office in his mind he was hearing "drive off the road" or "run into that pole." He shared with us that earlier in the day he had been banging his head on a wall, and I could see that his forehead was red and bruised. Jeffrey had a spirit of murder that had gained entry to his life through substance abuse. The spirit was getting very close to having his way with Jeffrey. He made numerous suicide attempts (Mark 5:1-6; Luke 9:39-42).

Physical Maladies

In addition to the symptoms of the demoniac in Luke 8, we often see sickness and disease (Luke 4:39; Luke 4:41; Luke13:10-1). Sometimes the disease is specifically stated as deafness or muteness (Luke 9:39-42), but more often a general summary is given.

Patrick came to us with symptoms of substance abuse. He was unable to overcome the temptation to use especially when he felt abandoned. As we prayed with Pat we found several sub-parts of his personality that were created when he was about six years old and felt he had been punished unjustly. His father had berated the boy for not paying attention and then stormed off in a rage leaving him abandoned for several hours. As Pat grew up he lost the hearing in his right ear. After we prayed and God healed prayer three or four parts, Pat's hearing was restored. We surmised that a curse had settled on one of the sub-personalities and we were able to remove it by inner healing followed by taking him through the Steps to Victory. (moriahfreedomministry.com)

Doctrines of Demons

Francis had experienced a very traumatic childhood, and I was concerned about working with her because of her spiritual commitment to the Jehovah's Witnesses. After trying to share with her the Christ of the Bible it became obvious that she would not receive the truth. I typically cut off counseling sessions like this, knowing that even if I could get the enemy to exit the Holy Spirit would not fill her. But I thought there was a chance I might be able to help her in a small way by leading her through forgiveness of the perpetrators who had abused her. Forgiveness is a universal principle for everyone, not just Christians. As we worked with her in inner healing we came across a sub-personality that was connected to a girlfriend who also was a Jehovah's Witness. As I led this inner child to begin to forgive her mother and her girlfriend, a demonic spirit manifested. Instead of just shutting the enemy down I commanded it to identify itself and reveal its lies. Remarkably, it was a Jehovah's Witness spirit and admitted that its doctrine was false. I did not have to share Christ with Francis because the demon's confession was enough to convince her. We were able to have Francis make a confession of Christ. As the doctrine of demons was revealed to Francis she came free (1 Timothy 4:1).

Chapter 4: 10 Myths of Demonization

In the course of ministry we hear many objections to Christian demon-possession (demonization). A wide variety of Christian authorities—commentaries, sermons, and radio programs—have offered various scripture passages and arguments that seem to refute the possibility of Christian demonization. If an afflicted Christian believes this, he or she will remain in bondage and not seek deliverance. In fact, in such cases the demonized believer will be victimized by the enemy as well as the church. I have found it useful to help people understand these Scriptures and arguments to remove stumbling blocks for these victims. It also helps to engage their faith fully in the process of deliverance ministry. In this section you will find the most common myths and biblical refutations.

> **Myth 1: Christians cannot be demon-possessed. A child of God is bought by Jesus' shed blood and therefore no Christian can be owned by the enemy.**

I have come to believe that the idea of demon-*possession* is misleading. Although many reputable theologians, pastors, commentators, and our most common English translations continue to translate the Greek word *daimonizomai* as "demon-possessed," I have discarded the concept after much study. Thinking of that hyphenated word paints a picture in my mind of a "demon owning or having a person." This common notion of demon-*possession*, however, is not supported by an examination of parallel accounts of demonization in the Scriptures. In fact, the opposite is the case: the person *possesses* or *has* a demon.[5]

Take Mark 7:25, for example, which reads "For a certain woman whose young daughter had an unclean spirit...." In the parallel passage in Matthew 15:25 Matthew used the Greek verb "daimonizomai," which has been traditionally translated "demon-possessed." It is apparent that the verb "daimonizomai" in this case does not carry the connotation of demon ownership since the Markan passage makes it quite clear that the *reverse* is true. When Jesus was accused of operating under the influence of a demon, the Pharisees did not accuse him of being "demon-possessed." Instead they accused Him of having (or possessing) a demon.[6]

In an important passage related to this issue John used the word "daimonizomai" in one sentence. In the previous sentence in the same paragraph John used the phrase "he has a demon." Clearly John was giving credit to the person as having the superior position (i.e., he possessed the demon; it didn't possess him).[7]

> "And many of them were saying, 'He has a demon and is insane. Why do you listen to Him?' Others were saying, 'These are not the sayings of one demon-possessed.'" (John 10:20-21)

The thrust of Scripture indicates that a demon can influence and pressure certain behaviors. But the person must, to some degree, submit to the guidance or direction of the unclean spirit. I will refer to this condition as demonization—not demon-possession. In his Bible Study pamphlet "Satan...The Occult," Chuck Swindoll shared the following observation.

> "There is no such word as demon-possession in the Bible. The word demonized, which means a person has a demon appears 13 times in the Greek and, in 12 cases, actually describes a victim...The extreme case of the demoniac in Mark 5 does not give evidence of total possession of this man by demons that indwelt him. This individual saw Jesus, recognized him, and desired to find help and release. A part of this man was still his own. He was simply 'demonized'—not 'demon-possessed.'"[8]

The word diamonizomai is used thirteen times in the gospels, seven times in Matthew, four in Mark, and once in Luke and John. A parallel expression echein daimon, 'have a demon' occurs once in Matthew, four times in Luke and five times in John. Luke and John use both of these words interchangeably. The rendering by English translators of 'demon-possession' confers too much control to the demon spirit.[9]

Chuck Swindoll goes on to say that the cases of demonization in Scripture do not depict an evil person following Satan. They do not even suggest that these people have committed great sins. We do not see Jesus or the apostles casting demons out of the Pharisees or Sadducees. Instead, many are innocent children who have been tormented since birth. Some are declared to be "daughters of Abraham" or otherwise identified as covenant children. This victimization does not seem to change as we move into the book of Acts where we find the Apostles still casting demons out of victims.

Chuck Swindoll makes this distinction to counter a popular but inaccurate teaching today that holds that non-Christians can be demon-possessed whereas Christians can only be demon-oppressed. As demonstrated clearly above the Bible clearly does not teach a "doctrine" of demon-possession and never speaks of demon-oppression. Not a single passage in the Scriptures teaches what demon oppression might be, nor have I ever seen a scripturally-supported doctrine of demon oppression versus possession. When someone attempts to describe "oppression" it usually ends up with something like this: *Satan is using another person.* While this is certainly one of Satan's ploys, it does not account for all the symptoms that victims share. The oppression that victims describe when they come in for help is not *outside* their person, but rather *inside.* They are describing voices, deep-level emotional manifestations, and physical and mental illnesses.

The Bible speaks of only one condition—demonization. This condition might be mild, as in the case of Paul, or intense, as in the case of the demoniac of the Gerasenes. The "false doctrine" of demon oppression is an attempt on the part of those who do not believe that a Christian can be demonized to resolve the dilemma presented by those real-life cases in which Christians are displaying the same symptoms as a demon-*possessed* person. Although on its face this might seem to be a reasonable premise, I cannot quote a single theologian that has scripturally supported a doctrine of demon "oppression" versus "demon-possession."

So we ask: *What exactly might demon oppression be? Does it include thoughts or emotions? Could it be a "thorn" in the flesh? If it includes any one of these does that mean that the enemy has penetrated our temple?*

If it is not one of these things then exactly what is oppression? Is it an imaginary cloud? If demons can affect our thoughts and emotions they are not just "outside" but in some real way have entered into our being. We do not carry our emotions and minds in a wagon behind us. These aspects of our soul are *within* our "temple."

Another interesting point is that in no case in Scripture do we see a person released from demonization in order to share the Gospel. If demons were only cast out of unsaved persons we would expect to find at least one case in which, after the demon was cast out, the Gospel was shared as a logical next step in the process. This is especially significant in light of the fact that our main purpose in ministry is to seek and save the lost. Demonized people do not seem to be among the "lost" but rather to be believers exhibiting faith who are merely set free from bondage.

Another observation is that we do not see either Jesus or the apostles rebuking a person for his condition of demonization. Instead, as Chuck Swindoll points out, the demonized are treated as victims. Jesus and the apostles administered acts of mercy to them. In many cases the victims were small children or individuals who had suffered a particular affliction since childhood. This is the testimony of the biblical record.

Finally, the concept of demon-possession is *never* taught in Scripture. Possession means ownership. An unbelieving man is always presented as an autonomous being who makes his own choices. He is solely responsible for his choices and until the day he dies he is presented with an offer to repent. God Himself effects any hardening of the heart; it is never attributed to Satan or his forces.[10] God allows us to choose whom we are to follow and, therefore, *Satan never owns us.*

Myth 2: There is no evidence of church deliverances. A frequently asked question is: "Where in the New Testament is there an example of Christians gathering together to cast out demons?"

I would like to share two points. First, this is in part an argument from silence—because it is not seen in the Bible it is not doctrinally acceptable. This is not a valid measure for determining sound doctrine because by this standard we would have to conclude that there is no "scriptural instance" on which to base youth programs or seminars or worship services where a Senior Pastor brings a sermon to the congregation. Instead, we see gatherings at which many share (1 Corinthians 14:26). The truth is that we do many things that are not shown in Scripture because they allow us to edify the body of Christ.

The second point is that we do see some examples of this practice in Scripture. Read carefully the following passage from Acts chapter 5.

> "And all the more believers in the Lord, multitudes of men and women, were constantly added to their number; to such an extent that they even carried the sick out into the streets, and laid them on cots and pallets, so that when Peter came by, at least his shadow might fall on any one of them. And also the people from the cities in the vicinity of Jerusalem were coming together, bringing people who were sick or afflicted with unclean spirits; and they were all being healed." (Acts 5:14-16)

There is no indication or suggestion that these sick people were non-Christians. The apostles were casting unclean spirits out of all who came or were brought. Note that Luke reports the addition of new believers to the body as occurring before the healing and deliverance was performed. In addition to the many examples of deliverance reported in the Gospels and Epistles, there is also clear evidence that exorcisms were practiced in the early church. The following translations of accounts from the early church use the word "exorcism" where I have used the term "deliverance." The words refer to the same practice. In fact, the process of exorcism/deliverance described in the early church is virtually identical to the one we use today.

In the early church, there was an office of exorcist that included deliverance. The following is an example.

> "I salute the holy presbytery. I salute the sacred deacons, and that person most dear to me, whom may I

behold, through the Holy Spirit, occupying my place when I shall attain to Christ. My soul be in place of his. I salute the sub-deacons, the readers, the singers, the doorkeepers, the laborers, <u>the exorcists</u>, the confessors. I salute the keepers of the holy gates, the deaconesses in Christ. I salute the virgins betrothed to Christ, of whom may I have joy in the Lord Jesus. I salute the people of the Lord, from the smallest to the greatest, and all my sisters in the Lord."[11] [emphasis added]

The practice of exorcism was actually a precursor to baptism. In the following passage we see exorcism expressed as a prerequisite to entrance into the fellowship of believers. Many "Early Church Fathers" describe the following ordinance with only slight variations.

"Crescens of Cirta said: In such an assembly of most holy fellow-priests, as the letters of our most beloved Cyprian to Jubaianus and also to Stephen have been read, containing in them so much of the holy testimonies which descend from the divinely made Scriptures, that with reason we ought, all being made one by the grace of God, to consent to them; I judge that all heretics and schismatics who wish to come to the Catholic Church, shall not be allowed to enter without they have <u>first been exorcised</u> and baptized; with the exception of those indeed who may previously have been baptized in the Catholic Church, and these in such a way that they may be reconciled to the penitence of the Church by the imposition of hands."[12] [emphasis added]

Those who practiced exorcism were considered to have received a special gift from God. They were held in high esteem and were to be ordained if the occasion arose.

"I the same, make a constitution in regard to an exorcist. An exorcist is not ordained [his office doesn't come from men]. For it is a trial of voluntary goodness, and of the grace of God through Christ by the inspiration of the Holy Spirit. For he who has received the gift of healing is declared by revelation from God, the grace which is in him being manifest to all. But if there be occasion for him, he must be ordained a bishop, or a presbyter, or a deacon."

The early Church acknowledged exorcism of new converts as an induction rite into the Christian faith. The same author further expounded on exorcism:

"Accordingly, when an exorcist was ordained the bishop was directed to give him the book in which the exorcisms were written, with the words, 'Receive thou these, and commit them to memory, and have thou power to lay hands upon Energumens, whether they be baptized or only Catechumens.' Though this Canon speaks only of exorcising Energumens, or such persons as were supposed to be possessed by evil spirits, we must remember that the power of such spirits was believed to extend to the whole world outside the Christian Church. Thus all converts from paganism and Judaism, and even the children of Christian parents were exorcised before being baptized. The practice was closely connected with the doctrine of original sin, as we see in many passages of St. Augustine, and is declared by him to be very ancient and universal. In expounding the Creed to candidates for Baptism, he says: 'Therefore, as you have seen this day, and as you know, even little children are breathed on and exorcised, that the hostile power of the devil may be driven out of them, which deceived one man in order that he might get possession of all men.'"

The emphasis placed on the need for exorcism implies that, if the rite was not followed, a Christian might still have demonic spirits. **Baptism into the faith was never seen as automatic protection from the spiritual realm**.

We also have an extant copy of an exorcism attempted without invoking the power of Christ's name. I include it because it conjures a rather humorous mental picture.

"They said, 'Oh, we will cast him out.' They put their hands upon him, and they tried to do it; but they whispered among themselves and said, 'We are afraid we shall not be able.' By-and-by the diseased man began to froth at the mouth; he foamed and scratched the earth, clasping it in his paroxysms. The demoniac spirit within him was alive. The devil was still there. In vain their repeated exorcism, the evil spirit remained like a lion in his den, nor could their efforts dislodge him. 'Go!' said they; but he went not. 'Away to the pit!' they cried; but he remained immoveable. The lips of unbelief cannot affright the Evil One, who might well have said, 'Faith I know, Jesus I know, but who are ye? ye have no faith.' If they had faith, as a grain of mustard seed, they might have cast the devil out; but their faith was gone, and therefore they could do nothing."

This account of an unsuccessful attempt at exorcism is eclipsed by accounts of many successful Christian exorcisms found throughout the literature of the early church.

The literature of the church provides abundant evidence of demonic expulsions within the body of Christ. Exorcism was an integral part of the early church rituals. New believers were subjected to deliverance after they confessed faith in Christ but before the rite of baptism was administered.

Myth 3: Our temple can have only one spirit. Paul, writing to the Corinthians, said that our bodies are the temples of the Holy Spirit who is in us (1 Corinthians 6:19; 1 John 1:1-4; John 2:19-21). If the Holy Spirit is in our temple then no other spirit can reside within us.

In this section we have quoted many passages that seem to portray an image of the Christian housed within a protective bubble—the "the temple." As we shall see, however, the Scriptures that allegedly prove this position of Christian protection from "demon-possession" cannot stand up to contextual scrutiny.

The contention is that the Holy Spirit and an evil spirit cannot reside in the same temple (body). So let's examine whether this conclusion is supported by the temple analogy that Jesus, John, Peter, and Paul used. Jesus first made the connection or analogy between the temple and our bodies when He said "destroy this temple and in three days I will raise it up." Paul continued in this fashion to link our bodies to the Old Testament temple. Jesus' temple (body) never had anything unclean in it. Our temples (bodies), on the other hand, are very similar to the earthly temple.

A cursory study of the Jerusalem temple reveals that during the time of the prophets Jeremiah and Ezekiel the temple contained detestable idols and all sorts of abominations. Ezekiel chapters 8 and 9 are devoted entirely to the imagery of God residing in a temple that is detestable to Him.

> "And He said to me, 'Son of man, do you see what they are doing, the great abominations which the house of Israel are committing here, that I should be far from My sanctuary? But yet you will see still greater abominations.' Then He brought me to the entrance of the court, and when I looked, behold, a hole in the wall. And He said to me, 'Son of man, now dig through the wall.' So I dug through the wall, and behold, an entrance. And He said to me, 'Go in and see the wicked abominations that they are committing here.' So I entered and looked, and behold, every form of creeping things and beasts and detestable things, with all the idols of the house of Israel, were carved on the wall all around. And standing in front of them were seventy elders of the house of Israel, with Jaazaniah the son of Shaphan standing among them, each man with his censer in his hand, and the fragrance of the cloud of incense rising. Then He said to me, 'Son of man, do you see what the elders of the house of Israel are committing in the dark, each man in the room of his carved images? For they say, "The LORD does not see us; the LORD has forsaken the land."' And He said to me, 'Yet you will see still greater abominations which they are committing.' Then He brought me to the entrance of the gate of the LORD'S house which was toward the north; and behold, women were sitting there weeping for Tammuz. And He said to me, 'Do you see

this, son of man? Yet you will see still greater abominations than these.' Then He brought me into the inner court of the LORD'S house. And behold, at the entrance to the temple of the LORD, between the porch and the altar, were about twenty-five men with their backs to the temple of the LORD and their faces toward the east; and they were prostrating themselves eastward toward the sun." (Ezekiel 8:6-16, emphasis added)

Ezekiel continued to describe the abominations and false worship desecrating the temple through chapter 16. His indictments against Israel were extensive, and we observe that during this period the Spirit of God departed from the earthly temple.

"Then the glory of the LORD departed from the threshold of the temple...." (Ezekiel 10:18)

Likewise, this Old Testament analogy applies to our New Testament temple—our bodies, the temple of the Holy Spirit. We are commanded to stop sinning and be filled with the Spirit. Why? Because we can have a detestable temple! Though I am not suggesting that the Holy Spirit would depart from a Christian based on sins committed, I *am* submitting that the Spirit can be quenched by our behavior.[13]

Jesus, John, Peter, and Paul all used the imagery of the temple to describe our physical bodies. It is therefore valid to use this imagery of the Jerusalem temple in comparison to our own bodies. The assumption that no other spirit beside the Holy Spirit can dwell within a believer's temple (body) is only a partial truth. It is *not* the whole truth revealed in Scripture.

To understand this problem let us return to the full imagery of the Jerusalem temple. The temple had two compartments. One compartment was the Holy of Holies. The High Priest alone was permitted to enter that compartment once a year and only after he had met the high standards of ritual cleanliness prescribed in the Scriptures. A rope was even tied to the High priest's feet so that, if he were unclean or in sin and died upon entering the Holy of Holies, he could be pulled out of this most holy place. Any other person who approached the Holy of Holies would meet with instant death.

Many priests were admitted to the outer portion of the temple area where the table of shew bread, the candelabra, and bowl of incense were kept. This was the area of the temple that Ezekiel described as being desecrated by abominations carved into the walls. Demons and idols of every form of pagan worship had been allowed to enter this area of the temple. The Holy of Holies was still intact, but the outer portion of the temple was in a state of defilement. In the days of King Manasseh the temple was defiled in a similar way.

> "He did evil in the sight of the LORD according to the abominations of the nations whom the LORD dispossessed before the sons of Israel. For he rebuilt the high places which Hezekiah his father had broken down; he also erected altars for the Baals and made Asherim, and worshiped all the host of heaven and served them. He built altars in the house of the LORD of which the LORD had said, 'My name shall be in Jerusalem forever.' For he built altars for all the host of heaven in the two courts of the house of the LORD."
> (1 Chronicles 33:2-5)

As we consider this imagery, let us follow the example of the New Testament writers and compare it to our own bodies. Is our temple (body) in the Spirit or is the Spirit in the body? Our body is not holy, but the Spirit that seals us is! Just as God did not choose the earthly temple in Jerusalem as His permanent home, so our bodies will not be redeemed. Just as there is a heavenly temple where God dwells, so we will have a heavenly body. Although our future glorified body seems to come from the same material as our old fleshly shell, according to 1 Corinthians 15 it is transformed.[14] God sees our fleshly nature as detestable, unholy, and unworthy of redemption. It is this condition that Paul wars against spiritually in Romans 7.

So, given the sin-fallen, unclean condition of our bodies, the question arises: Why would we assume that an unclean spirit could not enter or demonize an unclean vessel? Certainly we are no greater than Paul who could not gain spiritual mastery over his flesh. If we cannot take possession and have mastery of our bodies, how can we declare freedom from spiritual incursions into them? For Paul there was an issue of spiritual pride.[15] Could we, too, have an issue in our life that allows Satan to gain a foothold? How about unforgiveness, or envy (covetousness), or lust, or any other unconfessed sin?

The body-temple analogy reveals that the temple was composed of various compartments. The Holy of Holies was the area in which the Spirit of the Lord resided. The Spirit did not rest in any of the outer chambers or courts. This analogy suggests that a person can be demonized without having the Spirit within affected because of the separation between the Holy area (the outer chambers) and the Holy of Holies (the inner sanctum).

The temple imagery also suggests that, at least initially, the Holy Spirit does not possess the entire body. That is why we are called to be "filled with the Spirit." This is a command not a declaration. The filling is not the same as the gift of, or the sealing by, the Holy Spirit. Here is the difference:

- *Receiving the Holy Spirit* has to do with our justification and our acceptance of Jesus Christ as our Savior.
- *Filling by the Holy Spirit* is a process that requires our sanctification. It has to do with our walk.

Filling is our responsibility and a continuous process. We might achieve it one moment and then lose it the next on account of an act of disobedience. When we disobey God we quench the Holy Spirit. This is clearly the context of 1 Corinthians 6: 19 in which Paul declares the body to be the temple of the Holy Spirit. We merely have to back up one verse to see that Paul is identifying a mode of behavior that protects us from the enemy. His charge is "flee immorality." The consequence of continuing to sin is that our "temple" becomes defiled. Whenever there is a stated consequence there must be a potential transgression.

> "Flee immorality. Every other sin that a man commits is outside the body, but the immoral man sins against his own body." (1 Corinthian 6: 18)

Far from proving that a Christian cannot be demonized, this passage of Scripture teaches that we *can* and *do* defile ourselves. We are commanded to flee from immoral defilement, but we are not taught the consequences of this defilement. Paul began this section of Scripture with a warning:

"Or do you not know that the one who joins himself to a harlot is one body with her? For He says, 'The two will become one flesh.'" (1 Corinthians 6:16)

Just as a Christian can defile his body by joining it to a harlot, so he can defile his body by joining it to a demonic empowerment. If we believers could *not* do this Paul would have had no need to warn us about our behavior. Paul even cautions us against receiving a different spirit from the Holy Spirit.

"For if one comes and preaches another Jesus whom we have not preached, or <u>you receive a different spirit which you have not received</u>, or a different gospel which you have not accepted, you bear this beautifully." (2 Corinthians 11:4, emphasis added)

Myth 4: A Christian cannot fellowship with darkness. ". . . what communion light has with darkness, and what concord Christ has with Belial and what agreement the Temple of God with idols?" (2 Corinthians 6:14-16)[16]

This is another Scripture often cited as proof that a Christian cannot be demonized. Although this passage teaches that we *should not* commune with darkness, Belial, or idols, it does not teach that we *cannot* commune with them. In fact the passage teaches the exact opposite. If it were not possible to commune with darkness, Belial, and idols why would Paul have to tell us not to do these things? Instead, he boldly admonishes us to "Stop sinning," is Paul's admonition. This is not a Scripture that teaches that we cannot do these things.

Let's examine the verse in its full context:

"Do not be bound together with unbelievers; for what partnership have righteousness and lawlessness, or what fellowship has light with darkness? Or what harmony has Christ with Belial, or what has a believer in common with an unbeliever? Or what agreement has the temple of God with idols? For we are the temple of the living God...." (2 Corinthians 6:14-16)

The complete context of this Scripture makes it clear that we Christians do these very things. Many Christians reading these words find themselves in an *unequally-yoked* circumstance. Some may have accepted Christ after marriage or made a poor spiritual choice of a partner. Others may be participating in unbiblical activities because of job situations.

Many people contend that God and Satan cannot be in the presence of each other. That is not true, for Satan still has access to the throne of God and, according to Revelation, he is there day and night (Revelation 12:10). Similarly, a Christian can have both the Holy Spirit and a demon. The consequence of doing so is that there will be no harmony.

The fact that our bodies are a temple of the Holy Spirit does not provide impenetrable protection either. We saw above that God allowed evil spirits and demonic idol worship in the temple of God in Jerusalem. Ezekiel 8 reports that these detestable abominations were present in the "Holies" while the Spirit of God still inhabited the "Holy of Holies." In other words, just as the Israelites were allowed to defile the Jerusalem temple, so we Christians can allow defilement in our "temple" bodies.

This passage from 2 Corinthians does not teach that an unholy yoking of demons and the Holy Spirit is impossible. Rather, it warns us against such behavior. If it were impossible no such warning would be necessary (or make sense). Paul was asserting item by item that these things were not only possible but were occurring among Christians in the Corinthian church. His admonition was: *Stop it!*

"Therefore come out from them and be separate...." (2 Corinthians 6:17)

Paul leaves open the question "What happens when we do not obey the Lord?" Just because Paul commanded the Corinthians (and by extension all Christians) to "come out" does not mean that all have obeyed. Through the centuries since Paul wrote his letter to the Corinthians countless Christians have been unaware of God's commands or willfully disobeyed Him. I know that every person reading these words has, at some time, disobeyed God's will. Just because God has commanded us to do something does not mean that we always obey Him. Often we do not.

In my counseling experience this *unequal yoking* in sin, occult practices, or worldly pursuits is precisely what opens the door to bondages. Many Christians, after accepting Jesus as their Savior, still have their palms read or go to their astrologer for their horoscope. In some cases, they consume controlled or illegal substances.[17] I submit that any of these behaviors can allow Satan a doorway into our life.

Another "proof text" for the argument that a Christian cannot be possessed by demonic spirits comes from Paul's first letter to the Corinthians.

> **Myth 5: Christians and demons cannot co-exist in the same body.** "You cannot drink the cup of the Lord and the cup of devils" (1 Corinthians 10:21).

The passage above teaches that although communing with demons is not desirable it is certainly possible. At the conclusion of the passage Paul acknowledges this possibility by mentioning a result of such improper behavior—"provoking the Lord to jealousy." The fact that Paul cited a consequence of such behavior precludes the idea that the event or condition cannot exist.

> "Or do we provoke the Lord to jealousy? We are not stronger than He, are we?" (1 Corinthians 10:22)

Paul's statement that "you *cannot*" in verse 21 does not relate to a person's ability but rather to his or her participation without God's intervention. Sometimes God's intervention is discipline, and His discipline might be to permit demonic invasion.[18] There are consequences for our behavior.

> **Myth 6: The presence of the Holy Spirit drives out demons.** "You are from God, little children, and have overcome them; because greater is He who is in you than he who is in the world" (1 John 4:4). This Scripture is often cited as evidence that the Holy Spirit who indwells us is greater than any demonic spirit and, therefore, no demonic spirit cannot exist within the body of a believer.

The advocates of this position typically admit that a Christian can be attacked but they call it "demonic oppression." In stating this qualification, however, they never offer a logical explanation of how a person might be "oppressed" in a way that does not include his or her internal being—mind, will, emotions, or flesh.

We Christians are born again, meaning there are two of us. Our new nature is filled with the Holy Spirit. I submit that a demonic spirit cannot inhabit that area. Our fleshly nature, which is our body, however, is still in the world. A demon *can* inhabit this area. Paul wrote about this internal division in Romans 7 where he described being at war with his fleshly nature.

> "For we know that the Law is spiritual; but I am of flesh, sold into bondage to sin. For that which I am doing, I do not understand; for I am not practicing what I would like to do, but I am doing the very thing I hate. But if I do the very thing I do not wish to do, I agree with the Law, confessing that it is good. So now, no longer am I the one doing it, but sin which indwells me. For I know that nothing good dwells in me, that is, in my flesh; for the wishing is present in me, but the doing of the good is not. For the good that I wish, I do not do; but I practice the very evil that I do not wish. But if I am doing the very thing I do not wish, I am no longer the one doing it, but sin which dwells in me. I find then the principle that evil is present in me, the one who wishes to do good. For I joyfully concur with the law of God in the inner man, but I see a different law in the members of my body, waging war against the law of my mind, and making me a prisoner of the law of sin which is in my members. Wretched man that I am! Who will set me free from the body of this death?" (Romans 7:14-24)

Our bodies are in the world *not* in the Spirit. When we do not submit ourselves to the will of the Holy Spirit our fleshly spirit and its carnal nature control our bodies. Our fleshly bodies are not even redeemable as they are still subject to the law of death. They return to the dust and have to be transformed in the resurrection to a new glorified creation.[19]

The context of the passage refutes the myth that the Holy Spirit will drive out all other spirits. John is telling us that our Spirit (God's Spirit within us) is greater than any spirit of the world. John also alerts us to be on guard so that we do not receive the message of a false spirit. This false spirit can come to us as a false prophet or as a counterfeit spirit impersonating God or the Holy Spirit.

> "Beloved, do not believe every spirit, but test the spirits to see whether they are from God; because many false prophets have gone out into the world. By this you know the Spirit of God: every spirit that confesses that Jesus Christ has come in the flesh is from God; and every spirit that does not confess Jesus is not from God; and this is the spirit of the antichrist, of which you have heard that it is coming, and now it is already in the world." (1 John 4:1-3)

Thus it is clear that this passage does not teach that we Christians are immune to receiving a false spirit. Instead, John provides us with a test to use to discern whether a spirit is from God or not. Neil Anderson and Mark Bubeck both share accounts of using this test for spiritual discernment. (Testing the spirits is so important in spiritual warfare that we devote an extended section in section 4.)

Paul warns of these spiritual impersonations in several passages. In 2 Corinthians 11:14 he says, "And no wonder, for even Satan disguises himself as an angel of light." In this passage Paul warns us to be aware that Satan will masquerade as one of Jesus' angels.

In another Scripture Paul warns us to not receive a different spirit from the one we have already received. The spiritual test in this case is the purity of the Gospel.

> "For if one comes and preaches another Jesus whom we have not preached, or you receive a different spirit which you have not received, or a different gospel which you have not accepted." (2 Corinthians 11:4)

> **Myth 7: Satan is disarmed and cannot afflict Christians.**
> "When He [Jesus] had disarmed the rulers and authorities, He made a public display of them, having triumphed over them through Him" (Colossians 2:15). This passage is used to teach that Satan is powerless against Christians because he has been disarmed and can no longer afflict us.

After the cross, Paul still says that we are at war and even details the ploys of the opposition and our spiritual weapons to do battle against them. In 2 Corinthians 10:3-5, Paul speaks of our present engagement as warfare. In the present age there is still active opposition to the Christian kingdom. In Ephesians 6, Paul specifically mentions "fiery darts" that need to be extinguished. Apparently Satan has not yet been stripped of the fiery darts or his desire to wage war against the saints.[20]

How can Satan be disarmed and yet still have weapons? My old mentor Walter Martin used to say, "When you discover an apparent contradiction, go to the context." The fuller context of Paul's letter to the Colossians sheds light on this quandary. If we back up a few verses we see exactly what Paul was referring to.

> "And when you were dead in your transgressions and the uncircumcision of your flesh, He made you alive together with Him, having forgiven us all our transgressions, having canceled out the certificate of debt consisting of decrees against us {and} which was hostile to us; and He has taken it out of the way, having nailed it to the cross. 15 when he had disarmed the rulers and authorities, he made a public display of them, having triumphed over them through him." (Colossians 2:13-15)

In this passage Paul was speaking about the cancellation of the debts against us. The Greek word rendered "disarm" is more accurately translated as "spoils." Christ took the spoils from Satan and canceled the certificate of debts. In the Old Testament the power of sin was that death and separation from God were the consequence of sin. Christ paid all of our debts and, in effect, took us back as spoils from Satan's grasp. He did not place us in a bubble for our daily living here on earth, however. This passage relates to our eternal nature, the spirit within, not to our temporal fleshly nature.

Satan still has very effective weaponry in his arsenal, but it can no longer kill and keep us separated from God. Paul made this very point in Romans when he discussed the law before Christ's death on the cross and the effect of sin.

> "For sin, taking opportunity through the commandment, deceived me, and through it killed me." (Romans 7:11)

Satan's main weapon before the cross was his ability to tempt us to sin because when we sinned we were subject to the penalty for sin: death. This is the weapon that Jesus' work on the cross rendered useless. Satan can still tempt us and cause bondage, but for those of us in Christ the result is no longer death. After Paul made the point that sin brought death in the Old Covenant, he described the difference in the New Covenant.

> "There is therefore now no condemnation for those who are in Christ Jesus. For the law of the Spirit of life in Christ Jesus has set you free from the law of sin and of death. For what the Law could not do, weak as it was through the flesh, God {did:} sending His own Son in the likeness of sinful flesh and {as an offering} for sin, He condemned sin in the flesh." (Romans 8:1-3)

This is the disarmament or spoils that Paul was speaking about in Colossians. Satan still has weapons and can still inflict damage, but the wounds cannot cause eternal separation from God for those who are "in Jesus Christ."

Myth 8: If we are sealed by the Holy Spirit no other spirit can take possession. "For I am convinced that neither death, nor life, nor angels, nor principalities, nor things present, nor things to come, nor powers, nor height, nor depth, nor any other created thing, shall be able to separate us from the love of God, which is in Christ Jesus our Lord." (Romans 8:38-39)

Those who hold this view argue that our sealing by the Holy Spirit excludes demonic forces and, therefore, we cannot be separated from the love of Christ. This statement above seems logical until we examine the "proof text" passages that seem to support it in their proper context. The sealing by the Holy Spirit passage is actually in Ephesians not in Romans and describes the work of the Holy Spirit for our *future redemption* and not for our *temporal struggles*.

> "And do not grieve the Holy Spirit of God, by whom you were sealed for the day of redemption." (Ephesians 4:30)

The argument is that if a demonic spirit enters our life this means that we have somehow become unsealed. This argument is linked to the concept in Romans 8 that nothing can separate us from the love of God.

Here's the truth that the Scriptures support: *Even though we are sealed, an evil spirit can enter our life, but this does not separate us from the love of God.* In fact, we see both conditions in the passage in Ephesians in which Paul states that we are sealed: (1) we are sealed toward redemption but (2) we can still grieve the Holy Spirit by allowing demonic access.

This passage clearly separates our future redemption from our temporal Christian walk. It is only an *assumption*—not a fact supported by scriptural evidence—that sealing precludes demonic invasion.

In the fuller context of this passage, Paul has just warned us to not allow the sun to go down on our anger and stated a consequence of not abiding by the warning:

> "'In your anger do not sin': Do not let the sun go down while you are still angry, and do not give the devil a foothold." (Ephesians 4:26-27)

Therefore this passage clearly teaches that the devil might get a foothold in a Christian who is sealed. This is another of those passages that gets taken out of context and twisted to mean the exact opposite of what the author intended!

Myth 9: Only non-believers can have a demon. Some believe that demons can and do possess the bodies of non-Christians and that they can be delivered. They do not believe that a child of God has need of deliverance from demons.

First, I would like to challenge any of these authors to document a successful case of exorcism from a non-Christian. In thousands of cases I have never seen a full release unless the person has accepted Jesus and their will is engaged in the effort. (I prefer to call the process "deliverance" so that it is not confused with the Catholic rite). I would never attempt to deliver a non-Christian.

In Luke 11 Jesus states:

> "When the unclean spirit goes out of a man, it passes through waterless places seeking rest, and not finding any, it says, 'I will return to my house from which I came.' And when it comes, it finds it swept and put in order. Then it goes and takes along seven other spirits more evil that itself, and they go in and live there; and the last state of that man becomes worse than the first." (Luke 11:24-26)

Why would a demonic spirit find a "house" still empty upon its return? The conclusion that many commentators have reached is that the person was not indwelt by the Holy Spirit. They argue that the Spirit would naturally inhabit and fill a Christian in the areas that Satan and his forces have vacated. I believe the person referred to in Luke could only be re-occupied because he was unprotected by the filling of the Holy Spirit.

Further, this Scripture has caused me to back away from deliverance of non-Christians since my purpose in Christ is not to torment non-Christians but instead to desire that they come to Christ. In the process of sharing Christ enemies might be bound temporarily in a non-Christian but not "exorcised" or delivered. My entire effort with non-Christians is evangelistic and doctrinal. Casting out demonic spirits or commanding them to leave is reserved for those who are "in Christ."

During Jesus' earthly ministry (before He was resurrected), faith was a prerequisite for any healing including demonization. The actions and the requests of those who appealed to Jesus for healing or deliverance always exhibited faith. Jesus stated the need for faith on several occasions. In one case a centurion who asked Jesus to heal his servant expressed his faith that Jesus' word alone could heal the man.

> "But the centurion said, 'Lord, I am not worthy for

You to come under my roof, but just say the word, and my servant will be healed.'" (Matthew 8:8)

In other instances parents expressed faith in Jesus' capacity to heal their children. In a few cases friends demonstrated faith on behalf of their friends. In all of these cases we see that the person who was afflicted participated fully in the healing. They were submitting to and trusting in Jesus and the authority of their family members and friends. This is the context of deliverance in the New Testament.

> "And behold, a Canaanite woman came out from that region, and began to cry out, saying, 'Have mercy on me, O Lord, Son of David; my daughter is cruelly demon-possessed'.... Then Jesus answered and said to her, 'O woman, your faith is great; be it done for you as you wish.' And her daughter was healed at once." (Matthew 15:22, 28)

When Jesus gave authority to the apostles to go heal the sick and cast out demons, they were to stay in places where they were accepted. They were to preach, proclaim, and heal those who were willing. *Never in Scripture do we see the casting out of an evil spirit from a non-believer.* The Sadducees and the Pharisees (i.e., who were unbelievers) were never the objects of Christ's healing ministry. They were rebuked and taught but we never see them as the recipients of God's healing grace.

Now the question is: *If Jesus ministered deliverance to those who had faith before He went to the cross why would we want to change that doctrine and minister to non-believers after the resurrection? If Jesus asks for faith in Him can we ask for anything less?*

Knowledge and faith are essential if one is to experience complete and lasting freedom in Christ. Any person who receives deliverance and healing must have faith (if the candidate for healing is a child then a parent or guardian must exercise faith). Deliverance *always* comes by understanding the truth, and applying the truth through faith will set a person free. Without faith it is impossible to please God and receive His healing grace.

Even the demoniac of the Gerasenes, who suffered from what is arguably the most severe case of demonization in Scripture, was able to respond to Jesus in faith. When he saw Jesus he ran to Him and fell at His feet and began to implore Him (Mark 5:5).

> **Myth 10:** In the era of the New Testament demons cannot afflict Christians. There is a difference between the Old Testament and the New Testament with respect to demonic affliction. We Christians are under the New Covenant and are no longer subject to the same type of demonic affliction as those who were under the Old Covenant.

This position disregards the abundant scriptural evidence of demonization among those in a covenant relationship with God in both the Old Testament and the New Testament (i.e., the Gospels). Old Testament truths are not changed in the New Testament unless a specific proclamation is made. For example, we find that Old Covenant practices such as sacrifices, Sabbath days, offerings, and festivals were fulfilled in Christ. We read in the New Testament:

> "Therefore let no one act as your judge in regard to food or drink or in respect to a festival or a new moon or a Sabbath day—things which are a {mere} shadow of what is to come; but the substance belongs to Christ." (Colossians 2:16-17)

> "For the Law, since it was {only} a shadow of the good things to come {and} not the very form of things, can never by the same sacrifices year by year, which they offer continually, make perfect those who draw near." (Hebrews 10:1)

> "One man regards one day above another, another regards every day {alike.} Let each man be fully convinced in his own mind." (Romans 14:5)

These rituals are no longer necessary because their purpose was to demonstrate our need of and prophetically point to Jesus Christ. Paul says that the law was a schoolmaster to teach us about the reality of our sinful nature. He also teaches us which of the rites and practices can be put aside because their purpose was fulfilled in Christ.

By contrast there are no direct statements concerning a change in or cessation of demonic affliction or attachment from the Old to the New Testament. As we have discovered in examining the previous myths in this section when we study the Scriptures in their full context we find no scriptural support for a new doctrine, transition, or different teaching.

To interpret the Scriptures cited in the previous sections as "proof" that a Christian cannot be demonized is only possible if one brings to the task of interpretation certain presuppositions. The Scriptures considered in their full context do not support the notion that a Christian cannot be demonized. One such presupposition is "two spirits cannot occupy the same body." This doctrine is refuted directly by the story of the demoniac of the Gerasene who had more than 2,000 demonic spirits. The contention that it is not possible for one of these spirits to be the Holy Spirit is based *not on Scripture* but only on a presupposition that assumes that when a Christian is indwelt his entire body is filled and cannot have an additional spiritual resident. Yet we know from Scripture that we are to be filled with the Holy Spirit, which implies that we sometimes are not filled. We also know from Scripture that the Spirit within us can be quenched. When we are not filled or the Spirit is quenched a demonic spirit can invade our old carnal nature. This is especially likely when a person is in habitual sin.

At this point we have demonstrated that there is very little scriptural evidence suggesting that a Christian cannot be demonized. The evidence offered by the opposing viewpoint takes the form of innuendoes, assumptions and, sometimes, Scriptures taken out of context to support a presupposition.

In the next chapter we will present the evidence of Christian demonization and the fact that the New Testament Scriptures include ample support for the view that a Christian can indeed be demonized.

Chapter 5: Christians Can Be Demonized

Although this issue is hotly debated among various Christian authorities, I firmly believe that a Christian can in fact be demonized. By "demonized" I mean *influenced physically and emotionally and deceptively guided*. In this section I will be presenting evidence that a Christian can be demonized.

It appears that the Apostle Paul, himself was demonized. In 2 Corinthians 12:7 the Scripture records that Paul received a "thorn in the flesh," a "messenger of Satan" because of the revelations he had received. Because of an issue with pride Paul would always have a physical infirmity *caused by a satanic spirit* to keep him humble.

> "And because of the surpassing greatness of the revelations, for this reason, to keep me from exalting myself, there was given me a thorn in the flesh, a messenger of Satan to buffet me—to keep me from exalting myself!" (2 Corinthians 12:7)

For many years I had studied the Word, and though I had read this passage countless times I had not connected the "thorn in the flesh" with "a messenger of Satan." A messenger of Satan is a demonic spirit. The word "messenger" Paul used in this passage in 2 Corinthians is the same Greek word that is translated "angel" in more than 180 occurrences. Many expositors spiritualize Paul's "thorn in the flesh." Some speculate that the Paul's "thorn" referred to those individuals and parties who opposed his teaching and the clear Gospel of Jesus Christ. This is a very tenuous position to take, however. If we do not take this passage as literal—meaning exactly what it says, then which passages are we to take as true doctrines and which ones are we to spiritualize? The thorn presented in this passage refers to a weakness in Paul that seems to be physical and internal, not external (i.e., Paul's human enemies). Internal refers to the "temple" of his body, soul, and spirit. This "thorn" at the very least penetrated Paul's body.

The testimony of the early church seems to be in keeping with this literal interpretation. An early Christian writer named Irenaeus (who lived less than 100 years after Paul, circa 130-160 A.D.) referred to it as an infirmity. Many speculated about Paul's illness and diagnosed him with a lame leg or a weakness in the eye. But not one of the early church fathers attempted to spiritualize the "thorn" in Paul's flesh.

If Paul the apostle, whose letters fill more than half of the New Testament and who was arguably the most effective Christian in history, could be demonized, then certainly many of us who are walking a less righteous lifestyle might be subject to demonic invasion. Over the years I have prayed with countless pastors and their wives, ministers and missionaries, who have come free of demons using deliverance principles.

Another point to note about Paul's "thorn in the flesh" is that it was *not* given to him because he had unconfessed sin. Rather, it was given to him to *prevent* him from sinning. Therefore, we argue that God uses demonic spirits to perfect His children.[21] In fact, that seems to be God's core reason for allowing demonic spirits the freedom He does. From the very beginning demonic spirits have acted to expose us to temptation, which implies that God wants us to learn how to choose between right and wrong.

Some other authors have claimed that Paul did not bind, rebuke, or cast out this satanic messenger but rather simply prayed that the Lord would remove it. This is the common logical fallacy known as *the argument from silence.* The Scripture really does not describe Paul's technique in praying about the messenger. The Scripture simply does not tell us whether Paul issued commands or not. We do know that on three occasions he had tried to expel the enemy. We also note from Scripture that casting out demonic spirits sometimes requires prayer. It is not surprising that Paul simply referred to this time as prayer to the Lord because, after all, the Lord is the power in demonic expulsion.

> "And when He had come into {the} house, His disciples {began} questioning Him privately, 'Why could we not cast it out?' And He said to them, 'This kind cannot come out by anything but prayer.'" (Mark 9:28-29)

"Satanized" Believers

The Scriptures report three cases in which Paul handed believers over to Satan so that their soul might be saved. In his first letter to the Corinthians Paul noted a blatant sin occurring within the church. Here is his response:

> "It is actually reported that there is immorality among you, and immorality of such a kind as does not exist even among the Gentiles, that someone has his father's wife. And you have become arrogant, and have not mourned instead, in order that the one who had done this deed might be removed from your midst. For I, on my part, though absent in body but present in spirit, have already judged him who has so committed this, as though I were present. In the name of our Lord Jesus, when you are assembled, and I with you in spirit, with the power of our Lord Jesus, <u>I have decided to deliver such a one to Satan for the destruction of his flesh, that his spirit may be saved in the day of the Lord Jesus</u>." (1 Corinthians 5:1-5, emphasis added)

Paul makes it very clear that the person in question is a believer, a Christian who is sinning. Paul hands him over to Satan so that his soul may be saved. What does "hand him over to Satan" mean? I believe this is similar to the circumstance in Job in which God allowed Satan an opportunity to affect Job until sin was confessed and his behavior changed. In Job's case he was counted "blameless," but this referred to his justification or salvation in the Lord. Job was not sinless. His sin was pride and we see that when he confessed his sin it was released and he was restored.[22]

In the case of the man in the church at Corinth, Paul mentioned the issue in a later letter to the Corinthians (2 Corinthians 7:12) and noted that the man had repented and was restored to fellowship. Thus Paul's scheme of turning him over to Satan seems to have worked.[23]

Another account recorded in 1 Timothy involved two people who were teaching incorrect doctrine. Paul responded to them as he had responded to the situation involving the man in Corinth.

> "Among these are Hymenaeus and Alexander, whom I have delivered over to Satan, so that they may be taught not to blaspheme." (1 Timothy 1:20)

Again we see that Paul handed them over to Satan so that they might learn a lesson. Paul was not declaring that these individuals were not Christians. He wanted them to change their behavior. The purpose of handing them over was to teach them not to blaspheme.

The Holy Spirit in these Christians apparently did not preclude Paul from putting these people under Satan's hand. Although these three persons were clearly believers they were nevertheless given over to Satan's control. Though we are not sure what kind of effect Satan had on these Christians, it is probable that these were cases of demonization. In examining the Old Testament examples of Saul and Job, it is easy to imagine emotional, physical, and relational tormenting.

Satan Filled Their Heart

Another passage in Acts also seems to indicate an indwelling by Satan in believers. This is a difficult passage for many who assert that a Christian cannot be demonized. The text and context makes it clear why this is a problem.

> "But Peter said, 'Ananias, why has Satan filled your heart to lie to the Holy Spirit, and to keep back some of the price of the land? While it remained unsold, did it not remain your own? And after it was sold, was it not under your control? Why is it that you have conceived this deed in your heart? You have not lied to men, but to God.' And as he heard these words, Ananias fell down and breathed his last; and great fear came upon all who heard of it." (Acts 5:3-5)

Satan entered Ananias' heart. Many commentators have concluded that Ananias and Sapphira were not Christians. They reach this conclusion *not* because of the context but rather because of a predisposed opinion. The prelude to this Scripture makes it clear that they were believers, for the context was a discussion about the Christian body of believers that included Ananias and Sapphira.

> "And the congregation of those who believed were of one heart and soul; and not one of them claimed that anything belonging to him was his own; but all things were common property to them." (Acts 4:32)

Acts 5 begins with the transitional word "but," indicating that there was no change in subject. Luke was recording events within the church of which Ananias and Sapphira were believing members. As the account ends the church was in "fear." Acts 5:11 says, "And great fear came upon the whole church...." if Ananias and Sapphira had not been Christians the church members would have had no fear. Instead it would have been cause for great assurance. If it were this simple to root out non-Christians, believers would have no reason to fear wolves in "sheep's clothing." If the Holy Spirit would simply destroy any non-believer masquerading as a member of the flock it would make many pastors' or shepherds' jobs much easier!

The word translated "heart" in this passage is from the Greek word *kardia*. It means the emotions, feelings, or mind of a person. All of these aspects are internal—within the temple. Satan penetrated Ananias and Sapphira's "temple" and caused them to follow his will and not keep the promise they had made to God.

Another thought-provoking consideration relates to the family. Satan attacked both of these people simultaneously. If one of the two had stood strong perhaps both could have withstood temptation. Similarly, Adam and Eve were tempted separately but were both taken down together with a common issue. Peer pressure and the "mob" mentality usually bring us down to our lowest level. The issue that caused both Ananias and Sapphira to fall is a common one. Not unlike Adam and Eve, Satan will use an individual to bring down others.

A Different Spirit

> "But I am afraid, lest as the serpent deceived Eve by his

craftiness, your minds should be led astray from the simplicity and purity of devotion to Christ. For if one comes and preaches another Jesus whom we have not preached, or you receive a different spirit which you have not received, or a different gospel which you have not accepted, you bear this beautifully." (2 Corinthians 11:3-4)

Paul is warning us that Christians can be led astray through spiritual temptation. He cites Satan and Eve as an example. The spirit Eve received was not in human form. Satan is real, but he is a spirit. An evil spirit, not the Holy Spirit, can come to us bearing a false doctrine. We need to examine our thoughts and emotions constantly to see if they are in agreement with the Gospel and true doctrine concerning Jesus Christ.

The purity of our doctrine is exemplified by our devotion to Jesus Christ. Satan causes us to focus on our kingdom versus God's kingdom. Good questions to ask about our ministries might be: *Are we more concerned with physical wealth? Are we more concerned with what we can get from God? Are we more concerned about a new prophecy? Are we more excited about where the newest doctrine is coming from?* These are the areas where Satan often tempts believers. Paul's warning is that we need to examine the purity of our doctrine to ensure that we have not received a false doctrine from a demon.

Grace and the Law

One of the more confusing issues concerning demonization is the meaning of being "free from the law." How can a demonic spirit have power over a Christian's life if he is free from the penalty of sin through Jesus' shed blood on the cross? Since Christ died for our sin what possible "right" might an enemy have?

These questions have caused me to wrestle with my former theological model. In the past I naïvely believed that Christ's work on the cross canceled the power of the Law. Instead, Scripture reveals that the Law continues beyond the cross.

"Do not think that I came to abolish the Law or the Prophets; I did not come to abolish, but to fulfill. 'For truly I say to you, until heaven and earth pass away, not the smallest letter or stroke shall pass away from the

Law, until all is accomplished.'" (Matthew 5:17-18)

The duration of the Law is "until heaven and earth *pass away*."

In Hebrews, Paul spends some time addressing the topic of covenants. At the end of chapter 8 he seems to be saying that the Old Covenant (i.e., the Law) has passed away. Many commentators have come to this conclusion. Let us examine Paul's words carefully:

> "When He said, 'A new covenant,' He has made the first obsolete. But whatever is becoming obsolete and growing old is ready to disappear." (Hebrews 8:13)

He is clearly saying that the first covenant has become obsolete. The Greek word is very similar in meaning to the English word "obsolete." For instance, when we say that a computer is obsolete we mean merely that technology has advanced. The computer may still be functional, but it is no longer the "best" tool for the job. This is what Paul was saying about the Law, and his teaching is further clarified as the sentence continues with "ready to disappear." If Paul had intended to say that the old had passed away, he would not have had to qualify his words in this way. So Paul did not contend that Jesus' crucifixion had canceled the Old Covenant. In fact, we can infer the opposite interpretation—that what has not passed away still exists!

The Law Will Pass Away

The Law will ultimately pass away when God judges all of mankind. The Law will end at the White Throne Judgment at the end of the millennium. According to Matthew 5 it will cease to exist after the old heaven and earth are destroyed. The Law is still the basis both for temporal justice and for eternal judgment. We believers will not be saved on the basis of the Law, but those who have not received Christ through the New Covenant will be judged by the Old Covenant. They will be found wanting and sent into the "lake of fire."[24]

For Christians the Law is still partially in effect. The Law relates to our temporal existence, but it is not in effect over our spiritual existence. If a Christian commits murder he is judged according to law and may even lose his physical life. Ananias and Sapphira lost their lives when they sinned against the Holy Spirit. Although their souls were received in Heaven, their earthly vessel was lost. Thus, a Christian who continues to sin or commits a sin whose penalty is capital punishment may lose his life and yet still be saved.

King David in the Old Testament would be an example of a "murderer set free." David arranged for Uriah's death in order to take Bathsheba as his wife (2 Samuel 11:12-17). His confession did not negate the consequences of his sin. He suffered the loss of his child and never rose to the spiritual level of his earlier years.

Likewise, if a Christian sins, he is still subject to the penalties and disciplines of the Law. Among God's disciplinary measures is demonic invasion.

The New Covenant

The prophet Jeremiah looked forward to a New Covenant. The details of this covenant, like the passage above in Hebrews, are not fully realized today. While the new covenant has been extended to us, we can also see that the true fulfillment of Jeremiah 31 will not occur until the millennium.

> "'But this is the covenant which I will make with the house of Israel after those days,' declares the LORD, 'I will put My law within them, and on their heart I will write it; and I will be their God, and they shall be My people. ...' 'Behold, days are coming,' declares the LORD, 'when the city shall be rebuilt for the LORD from the Tower of Hananel to the Corner Gate. And the measuring line shall go out farther straight ahead to the hill Gareb; then it will turn to Goah. And the whole valley of the dead bodies and of the ashes, and all the fields as far as the brook Kidron, to the corner of the Horse Gate toward the east, shall be holy to the LORD; it shall not be plucked up, or overthrown anymore forever.'" (Jeremiah 31:33-40)

While this passage clearly refers to a New Covenant, the context points just as clearly to a time when Israel and Judah are both restored in the land of Israel after Armageddon has transpired and a New Jerusalem is built. It is a different Jerusalem from the one of our present day. The land itself will be changed, raised up, to allow room for a new Millennial Temple. The prophet Zechariah prophesied about this event and time-frame as well.[25]

Neither of the New Covenant passages we have reviewed precludes the demonization of a Christian. The first relates to the New Man, and the second has to do with millennial blessings. We live under grace, which extends to our New Spiritual being. We also live under the Law, which relates to our old nature. When we sin we are still required to offer a sacrifice. For the Christian, Jesus Christ's sacrificial death on the cross accomplished the requirement, but we must still confess our sins to activate the power of His sacrifice in our lives.

> "If we confess our sins, He is faithful and righteous to forgive us our sins and to cleanse us from all unrighteousness." (1 John 1:9)

When we Christians confess our sins the curse of the Law is removed. This applies to sin that we have personally committed as well to corporate sin. We still must confess the sins of our families, our nations, and any other common groups to which we belong. The Lord's Prayer is given with the pronoun "our" Father not "my" Father.

The timing of the removal of all curses pertaining to this world is revealed in both Testaments. These are often passages that are misunderstood to relate to our spiritual freedom.

> "And people will live in it, and there will be no more curse, for Jerusalem will dwell in security." (Zechariah 14:11)

> "And there shall no longer be any curse; and the throne of God and of the Lamb shall be in it, and His bond-servants shall serve Him." (Revelation 22:3)

The context and teaching of these two passages are clear. This curse will be removed at the end of this age, which is the same time that Jesus stated (Matthew 5) that the Law would disappear. Until that time we still have to deal with sin, curses, and confession.

God Sent the Demon

One last note concerning the afflictions that demonic spirits cause. In both the Old and New Testaments, God is in sovereign control. Satan can do nothing to one of God's children without permission. The book of Job clearly teaches this principle.

"So the LORD said to Satan, 'Behold, he is in your power, only spare his life.'" (Job 2:6)

Satan was requesting God's permission to tempt Job. God grants permission but with a certain restriction: Satan cannot take Job's life.

Another example of God's sovereign control over demonic activities is in the book 2 Chronicles.

"And Micaiah said, 'Therefore, hear the word of the LORD. I saw the LORD sitting on His throne, and all the host of heaven standing on His right and on His left. And the LORD said, "Who will entice Ahab king of Israel to go up and fall at Ramoth-gilead?" And one said this while another said that. Then a spirit came forward and stood before the LORD and said, "I will entice him." And the LORD said to him, "How?" And he said, "I will go and be a deceiving spirit in the mouth of all his prophets." Then He said, "You are to entice him and prevail also. Go and do so.""" (2 Chronicles 18:18-21)

God not only permits the deceiving spirit to go but also declares that it will be successful. The success of this spirit is not due to God's manipulation of human will. Rather, He foresees the hearts of these prophets and knows how they will respond. The people want to hear enticing words and will listen to the lies without testing the message or the messengers.

Another example is Saul.

"Saul's servants then said to him, 'Behold now, an evil spirit from God is terrorizing you.'" (1 Samuel 16:15)

After Saul rebelled against God he further fell into sin in relation to David. He became angry and jealous with David over the slaying of Goliath and allowed the sun to "go down on his anger."[26]

The following day an evil spirit from God came upon Saul, and God allowed it to remain the rest of Saul's life. We might speculate that Saul could have done something to get rid of the evil spirit besides merely enjoying the temporary relief that David's harp playing provided. If Saul had forgiven David and confessed his sin of jealousy, the "right" of the demonic spirit may have been nullified. This is speculation, of course, but it is consistent with the full doctrine of how we are released from bondages.

In the New Testament we find the following examples of God's granting or allowing an evil spirit to have access to a believer. Satan requested and received permission from God to sift Peter.

> "Simon, Simon, behold, Satan has demanded {permission} to sift you like wheat; but I have prayed for you, that your faith may not fail; and you, when once you have turned again, strengthen your brothers." (Luke 22:31-33)

In another passage Paul was faced with a messenger of Satan who was the source of his "thorn in the flesh." Regarding Paul's affliction we already discussed how God permitted this satanic invasion. God sent the demonic spirit and allowed it to remain for the purpose of perfecting Paul. This seems to be the reason that God allows spirits to afflict his children—to perfect and discipline.

Part II: Understanding Fortresses

James L. Hanley & C. Tracy Kayser

Chapter 1: Dissociation

What do I mean by "dissociation"? Though the term dissociation is defined differently in the secular counseling literature, I am using the concept as described by Richard Dickinson (*The Child in Each of Us*), Rita Bennett (*Making Peace with Your Inner Child*), and Charles Kraft (*Deep Wounds, Deep Healing*).[27]

To help explain the concept of dissociation I find it helpful to start with an understanding of Multiple Personality Disorder (MPD). Although the term MPD is no longer in favor among many in the mental health professions, it is a concept that laypersons can easily grasp. A number of books and movies have popularized MPD, beginning with the bestselling book and major motion picture *Sybil* in the mid-1970s and continuing to the present day with the television series *United States of Tara*. These capture the condition very accurately as I have seen it played out in many lives. Persons suffering from full MPD usually act out their lives in two or more distinct personalities. In some cases those personalities have such strong boundaries that they are unaware of each other's existence within the same body. Occasionally they can even lead separate lives with little interaction between each other. I have worked with several persons with this condition who lived in our home or attended our church.

Take for example a young mother we will call Mary who was trying to live out her life with this condition. She had two distinct personalities. One functioned as an employee and was very skilled at the clerical job functions of typing, filing, and similar tasks associated with specific work assignments. Another personality functioned as mother and cared for her children. This personality had various homemaker and mothering skills that enabled her to care for her children with cooking, housework, and a variety of other domestic activities. Though many women in the workplace juggle responsibilities of work and home, Mary was not simply wearing "different hats" at work and at home.

Mary's environment usually triggered the appropriate personality to surface in order to handle the specific demands of the situation. Mary was able to function very well *if* nothing happened to upset her internal system that kept Mary the Homemaker and Mary the Employee separate. On occasion when a co-worker or boss would ask a typical personal question such as "How are the kids?" Mary would switch, suddenly and often dramatically, from her work personality to her home personality. Her homemaker personality would emerge and share all the details about her children that the conversation required. When the conversation was over and the person left her presence, Mary would remain stuck in her homemaker personality and no longer able to function as an employee. She found herself unable to type or perform the other tasks that her work required. Unfortunately for Mary, this pattern repeated itself time and again in her employment history, and her inability to perform her work assignments at such times caused her to lose job after job. She could easily secure good jobs, but her switching personalities prevented her from keeping them. People like Mary typically have a very strong "protector" personality who will make the necessary adjustments. But even the best "protectors" sometimes fall short of making the necessary switches. (We will look at protector personalities a little later).

Mary's case is extreme and very deep. Each of her personalities is distinct and has a full range of emotions and mental abilities. In less extreme cases, relatively minor dissociations can cause more subtle symptoms yet be nearly as debilitating.

Fortresses

In 2 Corinthians, Paul provides us with a basic explanation of fortresses:

"For though we walk in the flesh, we do not war

according to the flesh, for the weapons of our warfare are not of the flesh, but divinely powerful for the destruction of fortresses. We are destroying speculations and every lofty thing raised up against the knowledge of God, and we are taking every thought captive to the obedience of Christ." (2 Corinthians 3:3-5)

In Ephesians 6, Paul declares that the purpose of spiritual warfare is to quench Satan's fiery darts. In this passage from his letter to the Christians in the Church at Corinth, however, we see another objective of spiritual warfare—to tear down fortresses. So what exactly are these fortresses? Well, first we see that they are composed of *imaginations and speculations.* Other translations use the terms *arguments and ideas exalted above God.* These translations capture the underlying meaning of the Greek words Paul used and lead us to conclude that there are unique distinctions in waging spiritual war.

Second, we note in the above Scripture that the fortresses we battle in spiritual warfare are *internal* not external. They are not battles waged in the physical world but rather in the mind, in the emotions, and in the physical aspects of the body that come under spiritual assault. People often look at the troubles (tribulation) in the world. When they feel as though everything is going badly they assume they must be under spiritual attack. In Scripture, however, we learn from Jesus Himself that the "rain will fall on the righteous and the unrighteous." While the enemy certainly can attack from without, the passage from 2 Corinthians tells us to look inward as well.

Third, we see that fortresses are thought patterns in our mind. For example, when I became a Christian at age 33, I had believed the theory of evolution that I had been taught. The programming of evolutionary concepts was (and still is) prevalent in schools, books, and other media. Hardly a day goes by that we don't hear some evolutionary concept being stated as factual and true.

As I began to read and study the Bible, however, my worldview began undergoing natural erosion in favor of the biblical worldview. My belief (or faith) in evolution was a stronghold within me that was gradually torn down after my conversion. It was such a stronghold in my thinking that as I read the creation account in the book of Genesis I was constantly faced with the possibility that the Bible was not totally true. It was imperative that I re-examine this belief system and thinking pattern so that my Christian faith could be strongly implanted in my mind and heart.

My co-author Tracy questioned at one point in her life whether she had been born homosexual. That belief that her same-sex orientation was genetically determined was a stronghold. As I shared with her and taught her from Scripture we broke that secular worldview with the truth of God's word. Though Tracy understood that the gay lifestyle was morally wrong, the more important concept for her to understand was that she was not created "wrong." Further, she had to find hope that God could make her emotions right. It was imperative that she understand this truth in order for her to be able to rethink her womanhood and sexuality.

In the 2 Corinthians passage cited above, Paul speaks of fortresses raised up *against the knowledge of God*. In other words, these fortresses can be so deep-seated and created so early in a person's life that there is a lack of awareness of God within the fortress. It might seem odd how even though we know God a part of us can be so walled off that it is shielded from His presence. The condition results from a combination of dissociation (fortresses) and demonization.

The following chart from Charles Kraft's book *Deep Wounds, Deep Healing* helps us to understand how this condition can manifest in a person's life.

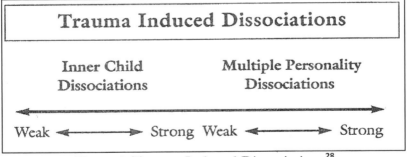

Trauma Induced Dissociations

Inner Child Dissociations	Multiple Personality Dissociations
Weak ⟷ Strong	Weak ⟷ Strong

Figure 1: Trauma Induced Dissociations[28]

Many of us in the counseling and pastoral care professions have found that this concept of dissociation can explain a wide variety of common psychology labels (or diagnoses) encompassing a variety of symptoms. The difficulties related to the dissociated parts of personality are almost always compounded by symptoms of demonization. Demonization will magnify the dysfunction. The combination of the depth of the dissociation and the magnitude of demonization is what causes a person to experience myriad symptoms that affect the mind/emotions, the body, and the spirit and result in a wide variety of diagnoses.

After praying with many persons who were later healed from some type of dissociative disorder I realized that they represented a number of preliminary diagnoses ranging from manic-depression, bipolar (mood swings), depression, and panic attacks on the milder end to psychotic disorders, paranoid schizophrenia in the middle and to full-blown Multiple Personality Disorder on the severe end. All such dis-eases that can be traced to dissociation can be labeled Dissociative Identity Disorder (DID).

Sub-parts or Sub-personalities

A number of different labels are used for this condition in Christian and secular literature—dissociative identity, inner child, soul pockets, parts, sub-personalities, flipsides, or alters. The terms are used interchangeably because they refer to the same underlying condition.

The parts have an identity, mind, will, and emotions separate from the core personality and will operate as a separate personality in relation to the core. I will refer to them here as "sub-parts" or "sub-personalities." All sub-parts carry either a traumatic memory or a coping behavior. Some will have very distinct walls of separation whereas others will nearly blend into the core. I will use the term "core" to refer to the part of the person that remains unaffected and is not a sub-personality.

In Multiple Personality Disorder (MPD) two or more complete personalities can co-exist in one person. In less severe cases of dissociation the sub-part will have a separate identity that becomes apparent in prayer and counseling yet never surfaces completely at the conscious level.

The chart above concentrates on trauma-related dissociations (for example, those that result from abuse or other traumatic experience). But it helps to understand that dissociation is a God-given ability we all have to focus our senses to a greater or lesser degree. For example, if I am driving down the street listening to a ball game on the radio and thinking about my next appointment and safely negotiating traffic patterns, I might be so engrossed that I completely by-pass my freeway exit. Or I might be watching a sporting event on TV and not hear my wife tell me that dinner is on the table even though she has spoken in a voice loud enough to for a normal conversation. My concentration on the game has masked (or tuned out) her voice. These types of dissociation are normal and even healthy because they do no permanent damage. By merely realigning our concentration we can return to normal communication mode with no aftereffects.

Trauma-related dissociations are another matter. These dissociations typically begin in childhood because many occurrences of severe trauma occur during our formative years. As children we are not equipped to cope with many emotionally and psychologically challenging situations and consequently a traumatic dissociation is created. Like Ann, many of us had parents who could not (or did not) keep the family unit together. Parental divorce, the death of a parent, or any type of abuse in the family can cause great and lasting damage to a child, especially if care and nurture are not given to help heal the wounds. Traumatic dissociation can result from a child's experience of physical or emotional abuse or abandonment or sexual molestation. Any number of events, real or imagined, may have combined in a child's life that lead him or her to be unable to process, understand, and (finally) cope with the challenges of life. By the time we reach adulthood we have acquired many life skills that help us to cope with situations of injustice and abuse, but as children we lack these resources. We do not understand how to heal from abuse and might not even have a real understanding of the world we live in. For example, a child might believe that he should be protected and that "God" should keep him from tribulation. But the truth that we learn as we mature into adulthood from both Scripture and personal experience is that people are not always rational or protective and that tribulation is certain and there is no such thing as a perfect life. In regard to protection God promises that He will walk through the tribulations with us—but not prevent us from its presence in this fallen world.

"These things I have spoken to you, so that in Me you
may have peace. In the world you have tribulation, but
take courage; I have overcome the world." (John 16:33)

Dissociation is a God-given ability to store memories, emotions, information, or abusive experiences in a safe place for a period of time until we (as children) reach adulthood and can finally deal with the experience."[29] For a Christian adult this will entail giving the memory, emotions, hurts, and traumatic experiences to Jesus. (We will examine this process in detail in a later chapter.)

Though no one is certain as to exactly how information storage works in dissociation, what seems to happen is this: A small part of the soul is compartmentalized for the purpose of storing the abusive experience along with the emotional hurts (you could think of it as a closet in a house used for storing things you don't want the company to see or a "junk drawer" that holds unsightly things). In some cases these "parts" are so walled off from the core personality that the core actually "forgets" the memory. In other cases the memory is known but the emotions associated with it are repressed (think of repression as a "lid that keeps them in"). In still other cases, it is just a pocket of emotions. In the case of MPD the different sub-personalities contain all the aspects of a soul, mind, will, and emotions (thus, it is no mere closet or pocket but a more or less complete, separate personality).

We often hear of people bringing repressed memories to light during counseling. Some of these "recovered" memories may be true while other "memories" are distorted or even false. When the latter occurs, and the person shares the distorted or false memories with other family members it can be very divisive. If this happens, the enemy can use it as part of his plan of attack to harm family relationships. The information needs to be tested. (We will deal this phenomenon and testing procedures in later chapters.)

Prevention of Dissociation

Parents and other caregivers can help prevent dissociation by offering the child who has suffered a traumatic experience(s) to share experience and release emotions. Fortunately many counselors have discovered this truth and crisis counseling is offered, for instance, after a school trauma such as a shooting incident or a building collapse occurs or even when a classmate is killed in an automobile accident or dies during a sporting event. The crisis counselors help children express and release their feelings about the traumatic experience. Allowing this time of sharing and open expression gives children permission and even encouragement to let their feelings out. Most dissociation occurs when the event is a "secret" that "must not" or cannot be discussed. The child then "stuffs" the feelings in the secret compartment. A typical situation is when a child is sexually abused and then told not to share it with anyone or even threatened with harm.

Four Types of Dissociation

In my experience four types of dissociations can occur. We used the example above to demonstrate a **trauma-induced dissociation**, which is by far the most common type. There are three other ways in which I have seen dissociation occur.

The second type results when a person **splits off a soul pocket over sin.** Sometimes a person participates in a sinful act or experience while part of himself chooses not to be involved. The person splits off a soul pocket to keep a part of his soul intact and "pure." Take Andrew as an example. He became a Christian in his early teens but later went through a rebellious phase. In high school and college he experimented with drugs. Andrew knew better and was conflicted internally over his duplicitous behavior so he created a part or sub-personality that was "pure." Whenever Andrew used drugs he suppressed this part of himself. Later whenever a sermon or Bible study would trigger this part of his personality, it would surface and accuse Andrew with shame and guilt. It would pounce on him emotionally and mentally. Andrew would obsess on Scriptures that indicted him for his sinful behavior and often doubted his salvation. He even contemplated suicide as a remedy to his torment. An antichrist spirit of legalism and perfection accompanied this sub-personality.

A third way I have seen dissociated parts created is when children **seek to memorialize a time in their life.** In this case they lock a part of their soul on a specific time in their life and refuse to "grow up." David was nine years old when his father accepted a job transfer to California. David was stunned. Leaving behind his best friend Billy broke his heart so David created a part to memorialize their friendship. This part never grew up and became a refuge of mental escape for David. Such parts as these are often difficult to discern because no trauma exists inside the part and as a result any unforgiveness or conventional sin is hidden. The problem arises because the separation from the core affords the enemy a legal right. David was experiencing difficulty in connecting with adult friends and having great trouble maintaining harmonious relationships. This occurred because the enemy would get involved. It is interesting to note that the enemy inserted himself in David's life exactly where David had sought to ensure a lasting friendship by memorializing his friendship with his best friend Billy—and prevented David from keeping a relationship. In fact, David could not keep a friendship to save his life. In a prayer session I led with David God kept taking him back to a picture of himself and his childhood friend. We finally discovered what the problem was by allowing the little boy part to share his story. As I asked the questions David could hear the thoughts from the nine-year-old part. We were able to heal that little boy and forgive his father, and God fused him back to the core. David now enjoys new friendships and is no longer afraid to open himself to deeper relationships.

The fourth type of dissociation is that **created in the womb**. When an ancestral spirit has been passed down from a former generation it can create a "flipside" beginning at conception. These spirits are the most powerful and malicious that we encounter. They tend to control the person's life and sabotage him or her at every turn. Because it can be the most troubling and confusing type of dissociation, we have devoted an entire later chapter to explain this condition more thoroughly.

Chapter 2: Bubble Theory

To understand how dissociation operates in a person's life I refer to a diagram created by Holly Hector, which I modified slightly to better reflect my understanding of the process.

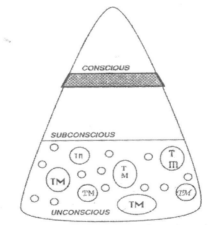

Figure 2 Trauma-Induced Soul Pockets[30]

In the above diagram the bubbles represent traumatic memories (TM). The diagram depicts three areas of the soul and, though I would be hard-pressed to defend the diagram biblically, I find it helpful in discussing how I believe the process works. When a child experiences a traumatic event that he or she cannot process emotionally, he or she often copes with it by splitting off a portion of the soul to encapsulate the hurts and sometimes even the memory itself. One woman I worked with labeled them "soul pockets." These TM pockets are then set aside or stuffed down to the lowest level of the soul—the unconscious portion depicted in the diagram. As long as the TM remains in the lowest area a person can operate in a fairly healthy way and deal with most issues and tasks in life.

The soul also seems to operate in three levels or compartments. The *conscious level* is where we perform most of our life functions. Just below the conscious level is the *subconscious level* that seems to be where we carry our emotions. In our daily lives we constantly experience our underlying fears, anxiety, or depression in this subconscious level. Below the subconscious is the *unconscious level* which is our storage compartment (like a cellar) and easily accessed for a variety of memories including TMs. Most of the time TMs stored in the unconscious level are in a state of suspension and do not manifest in many symptoms.

A problem often arises, however, when persons encounter situations that resemble or remind them of the previous abuse. At such times the TM bubble could begin to surface. As it rises to the subconscious level the person experiences the emotions and sometimes even memories of the previous abuse. In this state a person might encounter minor emotional difficulties, or if the TM pocket is large it may be completely debilitating. Panic attacks, depression, and anger might emerge with no apparent cause or provocation.

At this point it is fair to ask what purpose God might have in allowing this condition to occur. Although this discussion is speculative because we do not know for certain, we can draw some tentative conclusions. As children we have limited understanding of the world and its sin nature. Children are unable to understand and process many biblical truth-principles that seem to conflict with their life experiences. In other words, they have many false or unrealistic expectations about life.

When abuse occurs—such as rejection or ridicule, shame, isolation, abandonment, physical, sexual, or verbal abuse—and a child is unable to cope with it he or she can create a soul pocket. This pocket of hurts and attendant memories are encapsulated in a soul pocket (a TM bubble) and then suppressed down to the lowest level in the diagram—the unconscious level. The effect is that the core part of the person can continue to function more or less normally even though the hurt, pain, and memories have not been dealt with and released.

Instead, they are just placed in a holding area until the person matures enough to address the issues.

Secular counselors note that upon entering adulthood a child can no longer suppress these memories and accordingly certain triggering events will cause them to surface. From a biblical standpoint we believe that God is allowing this defense mechanism to cease its suppressing function so that the person can finally deal with the traumatic memories. We can refer to this as reaching the age of accountability.

Another way to think of these pockets is that they act as martyrs for the core. In other words, these pockets act to "save" the core personality until Christ comes into the person's life to take the burdens, memories, and hurts.

Triggers Summon Dissociated Parts

Another feature of these memory pockets in "saving" the core is that they may surface any time a person encounters a similar situation. When this occurs it is often called a trigger. Examples of triggers include a raised voice, a particular facial expression, a hurtful word or tone, or a specific temptation. *A trigger is anything that causes the dissociated part to think it is being summoned to carry a burden similar to that which caused it to come into existence.*

When a child is molested, for example, a part may be created to carry the memory and hurt of the experience. During every successive instance of molestation the part surfaces to carry further abuse. Instead of getting better over time, dissociated individuals tend to get worse because of the accumulation of traumatic memories being stored. Triggers multiply over several years of abuse and cause increasingly serious difficulties.

There is another significant problem with a dissociative soul pocket. Let us imagine for a moment that a parent verbally abuses a child, which leads the child to dissociate and create a part. Sometime later, when the child has calmed down and suppressed the part, the parent asks the child for forgiveness. The child's core personality forgives and is reconciled to the parent. The dissociated part, however, is suppressed and never either hears nor receives the apology. A child in this condition may grow to adulthood with an inability to forgive or release the hurt and pain that parent caused. The parent, on the other hand, will be unable to understand why the child is so angry and unforgiving and unable to let go of a past hurt.

Later in life this can create great difficulties in sibling relationships. One child, who may not have dissociated parts, remembers Mom and Dad as loving and caring while another child, who suffers from DID, remembers only the difficult times due to the surfaced part or soul pocket. One sibling tries to get the other to validate his "abuse," while the other cannot do so because he does not recall it being so difficult.

As a pastor I have observed another manifestation of this condition that goes like this. A church attendee hears the Gospel message and responds by coming forward to accept Christ. A few weeks later, after I have carefully led the person through a confession of the Gospel, he responds once again to the message at the end of the service and comes forward to accept Christ a second time. This might occur many times in the same church or at different times in different churches. Here is what is happening. While the person attending church is resting, worshipping, or listening to the Gospel message a part within him surfaces and wants to respond. As the person comes forward, however, the part is suppressed because of the new activity. So, when the confession is actually repeated (e.g., saying the prayer accepting Christ's gift of salvation), it is the core, not the part, who says the prayer and makes the profession of faith. The physical act of standing up and walking to the front of the church has caused the "unsaved" part to be suppressed once again. Often when I encounter individuals who respond to the Gospel message multiple times it is because they never feel "completely saved." The good news is that this changes when the person is healed of dissociation and feels whole, accepted, and fully God's child.

Pain, Anger, and Coping Parts

Let me share another phenomenon that I have seen occur frequently. A soul pocket may carry both the pain and the anger compartmentalized together. Many times, however, the pain, shame, and guilt will be held in one part. When that part is unable to release them an anger, rage, or frustration part will be created. When the child then stuffs these emotions, a third part can be created—the coping part. The coping parts are those that divert a person's attention from the other emotions (such as anger, shame, pain, and rage) that are not allowed or cannot be expressed. Coping parts are the ones that cause much of the person's dysfunctional behavior later in life including substance abuse, eating disorders, cutting, fatigue, running away, isolation, compulsive shopping, etc. The assignment of a coping part is to engage the person in any activity that serves to draw the person away from focusing on the pain.

When a pain part is triggered and surfaces it carries with it not only the emotions of the event the person is currently experiencing but also an accumulation of pain or anger (and other emotions) collected over the years of negative experiences. A pain part might bring with it deep depression or sadness. The emotions can be so debilitating that the person cannot even get out of bed. An anger or rage part may surface with such ferocity that the person can lose control and bust through doors and break windows.

The Protector

A coping part may be created to guard against such intense and uncontrolled reactions. Therefore while some coping parts function to distract a person from the pain, other coping parts may take on the assignment of protector to keep the intense emotions in check. The protector part assumes a dominant position over the other parts to keep them from surfacing and erupting in uncontrolled emotional displays. Protectors will most often be unemotional to the point of making the person seem emotionally flat and even "zombie-like" and fearful of change. Protectors will also frequently cause the person to be very controlling, and a spirit of fear may be allowed access that will accentuate this behavior. The protector is so determined to keep emotions in check that it will often stifle innovation in a person who is very creative and spontaneous.

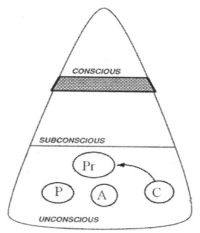

Figure 3: Classic Soul-Pocket Creation

The diagram above depicts this pattern. In a classic case all three parts will exist—pain, anger, and coping—and be presided over by the protector. Often there will be several parts in each category with slight deviations.

In addressing dissociated parts we must pay special attention to legal rights and strongholds. A **legal right** is what allows the enemy to come into a person's life and begin to affect the core personality and any sub-parts he or she might have. A **stronghold** is the lie that a person believes that allows the enemy to stay in his or her life. An example of a legal right is unforgiveness, which the Bible defines as sin. An example of a stronghold lie is believing that Jesus' work of salvation on the cross is for "everyone else but me."

When the legal right (sin) exists within a dissociated part, no amount or manner of confession in the core will seem to be effective. These people will also have great difficulty in owning and confessing an act that another part commits. "It wasn't me!" they would declare— even if the denied event was captured on videotape and produced as proof. *All dissociation works in this manner:* Each part denies that it is a part of the whole. Further evidence of this truth is that the part is almost always frozen in time at the time when the event the created the part (the dissociation) occurred. Thus the part does not grow up with the core. The parts are often in total denial that they are a part of the whole.

It is essential in understanding dissociation to see the sub-personality (part) as a legal right and not just a stronghold (lie). The legal right must be dealt with before the stronghold can be effectively addressed. Once the legal right has been dealt with, the stronghold that manifests as symptoms in the client's life can be broken.

Other legal rights might also exist within a part. For instance, the part may have been involved in occult activity. Or it may be a coping part, such as drugs or alcohol, that participates in sin as a coping mechanism. These legal rights must be expunged and dealt with by confession before we can move on to the strongholds.

Chapter 3: Tracy's Adult Struggles

Jim: When I began counseling Tracy, I wanted to get a sense of her struggles. I wanted to know her story—including information about her spiritual walk, family life, and emotional difficulties. I asked Tracy to start by sharing a short summary of her journey.

Tracy: I had been in Christian counseling on and off for 15 years and had spent more than $90,000 paying therapists to help me find an answer to my pain. For most of my young life into adulthood I had been in emotional pain trying to figure out who I was, why I had same-sex attractions, and wondering why I could not maintain any sort of dating relationship with a man.

At 16 years old I became engaged in a sexual relationship with my best friend's 21-year-old sister, which continued for three years. Nine years later I entered the gay lifestyle. I would enter one relationship after another, and each time the relationship ended I was devastated and felt like a child. Since I had accepted Christ as a child, in the aftermath of each relationship I would re-dedicate my life, resolve to try harder, attempt to pray and live in a state of hope … but I never got relief from the bombardment of sexual attraction and gay women approaching me. I lived in deep depression and emotional immaturity because I never had the opportunity for emotional stability and constancy. My life was turbulent, and the enemy capitalized on the fact that I didn't understand what was going on. I watched as my high school friends got married, had children, and led stable lives, and all the while I remained stuck in a "no man's land" in which I was unsuccessful in dating women due to the fact that it was not in harmony with my Christian beliefs but unable to date men because of the deep fears I harbored within. In fact, I used to believe that I was the one person who was truly "ambivalent" or "asexual."

I struggled through college and law school and eventually passed the State Bar Exam and began working as an attorney. I was so unstable emotionally that I had difficulty maintaining employment as a lawyer. I was a young adult … who felt like a child, a graduate student … who felt like a child, and a lawyer arguing in court … who felt like a child. No matter how mature or sophisticated I might have seemed as a professional, when I had to appear in court for a hearing I would cry the whole way there because I felt so young and was afraid to stand before the judge. The only way to soothe myself (I was not aware that they were inner parts at this time) in order to make my courtroom appearance was to call a trusted friend or my mother who would help calm me down.

Not only did I feel like a child but my emotions ranged from calm to rage, from security to insecurity, from happiness to depression, from hopeful to hopeless. I got no reprieve from the emotional turmoil or circumstances that would trigger it.

While in the gay lifestyle, I used relationships to mask the pain. I also entered psychotherapy to help me understand the dissonance between my Christian values and my gay lifestyle. I entered a process group (group therapy) for ex-gays with a Christian therapist who herself had left the gay lifestyle and married. While in this group, however, I befriended a female pastor and once again became entangled in a same-sex relationship—the very type I was trying to avoid. When my relationship with the pastor was exposed to our therapist the process group disbanded and the therapist tried to salvage my friendship with the pastor.

Once again I was faced with the challenge of trying to find help either from another therapist or anyone else who understood same-sex attraction and could explain why I was "stuck." During a 10-year span of my life I was in one gay relationship after another each of which always ended in a painful breakup that left me curled up on the floor sobbing in pain or in lying in bed for days on end feeling depressed and hopeless. At the time I did not know that demons were driving the severity of my emotions. I just thought I was broken beyond repair. I was not able to be gay and yet not able to be straight.

In deep emotional pain I sought help from no fewer than four Christian therapists, some of whom were gifted in spiritual warfare and others who where traditional talk therapists. I considered flying to

Colorado to seek the help of a well-known counselor who specialized in lesbian relationships. I went to a high-profile self-proclaimed exorcist and paid $500 for a one-hour session only to be told that I was a reprobate. I was seeking help not only for same-sex attraction but also because I was on a journey to heal the aloneness, the rejection, the abandonment, the wild shifts of emotion, and the feelings of "nothingness" that consumed me.

Jim: Aware that a lot of issues trace back to early childhood experiences, I asked Tracy about her family background and any traumas she might have experienced.

Tracy: I love both my parents and enjoy a close, transparent relationship with them today. My father was one of the best medical practitioners where we lived. He can be a generous man financially and gave my sisters and me a "well-bred" upbringing. My mother is an elegant woman. She was reared in Vienna, Austria, and taught us to speak German and made sure we traveled extensively, experienced art and culture, and spent a great deal of time with my sisters and me. This is the heart of who my parents are, and their own brokenness does not supersede their love for the three of us girls.

As a physician, my father worked six days a week and was thus both physically and emotionally detached from his family most of the time. My mother was 18 years younger than he and struggled with emotional unavailability based on her own upbringing and being married to a demanding husband and trying to raise three young girls largely on her own because her husband—our father—was absent.

I believe that from infancy I was unable to receive love and a sense of well-being because both of my parents were emotionally absent and our home-life was unsafe. I had a void inside and craved love, but I was also very afraid of rejection and isolation. My father was angry most of the time, and each day when he came home from work my mother and sisters had to test the air to see if Dad was in a happy mood or an angry mood. My father pitted us girls against each other and belittled us, which ignited turmoil in our family. As a result we were all in conflict with one another as adults and full of uncontrollable rage.

At times my father would sexualize and objectify women in my presence. This had a profound impact on how I felt about myself and my beliefs about men. I considered men to be unsafe and selfish and thought they expected women to cater to their needs, sexual and otherwise. My beliefs were twisted, and I had a distorted understanding of male-female relationships. I wanted nothing to do with men.

Jim: Tracy came to our church for the first time for a Thursday night Bible study. I met and talked with her after the study. Though on the surface she seemed to have it all together, as she shared her story it became clear to me that she was deeply troubled. In fact, I was amazed that she seemed to be so highly functioning. Tracy probably experienced over 50 percent of the dissociative symptoms on our list. In addition to dissociation, I detected demonic intrusion as she shared her story with me. Yet on the surface she had the elegance of a model and the keen intelligence we normally associate with members of the legal profession.

What most impressed me about Tracy's story was her spiritual tenacity. So many others would have given up. But Tracy pressed on through incredible opposition and found Moriah Counseling Ministry and ultimately her freedom. That tenacity combined with her heart for God made her a very attractive seeker to counsel.

As we talked I suspected that there was not going to be a quick solution for Tracy's issues. I knew that it would be an uphill struggle. So much of her story seemed to beg for deep inner healing. Longstanding struggles at home with her father and sisters and years of participating in the gay lifestyle (she was in fact involved at that time in a dysfunctional relationship) had left her deeply wounded.

As I listened to Tracy's story I realized that other important people were affecting her life, and I asked her to share information about her other significant relationships.

Tracy: The void inside left me starved for loving connection, and at the age of 16 I fell in love with my best friend's older sister, Char, who was 21. The relationship lasted three years. Although my mother constantly told me that she loved me, I remember driving down the street at 16 saying to myself: "I am finally loved." I first experienced sexual contact in my relationship with Char. And this sexual relationship opened a door to the enemy's influence. My sexual preferences and desires greatly changed at this time. From birth I was predisposed to have emotional and sexual attractions toward women. When I engaged physically with Char the predisposition was fully realized.

After I graduated high school, Char got married, and I attended a nearby college trying to muddle through the pain of life without her as many sub-parts of my personality were grieving and experiencing profound loss.

Years later, when I was 26 years old, Char's sister got married. Not knowing of our former relationship she booked me and Char in the same hotel room that had only one bed. By that time I had succeeded in shoved the emotional pain over the loss of Char down so far (in my sub-parts) that I was free from having to address the loss. But that evening a monster was unleashed, and I spent the next year and a half grieving the loss of my relationship with Char and trying to win her back. That event triggered my entrance into the gay lifestyle, and I believed Char when she said I was gay. I was not mature enough to listen to what my own heart was telling me that I wanted in my life.

Jim: I was interested in Tracy's family background, especially as it related to sexual partnerships. There is often a connection between someone's personal struggles and family history.

Tracy: I recently discovered that in my family of origin an aunt, an uncle, and several cousins were gay. Several of the deliverance ministers I went to had also suspected a generational spirit of homosexuality that came down my family line along with sexual dysfunction, fear of men, misogyny, and other family issues. They believed that I inherited a generational spirit of homosexuality that influenced my perception of life in general and men in particular and influenced greatly the choices I made about how to live my life.

Chapter 4: Symptoms of Dissociation

Over the years I have encountered thousands of cases of dissociation in my ministry. In this chapter I will summarize the major symptoms of dissociation. Demonization and dissociation are closely related because demonic spirits are often involved whenever a person is suffering from dissociation. The main difference between a person who is demonized and one who is dissociated is that a dissociated believer will often be unable to come free using standard spiritual warfare prayers and techniques. The person will often describe their symptoms with a mix of wounding, victimization and demonization. These individuals will often present as strong, mature Christians many of whom will report having attempted deliverance on many occasions with either no success or only temporary relief.

Nearly all such Christians will also experience some level of demonization that is associated specifically with the affected sub-part. The most common cause of demonization is unforgiveness, which comes with a biblical warning of demon affliction (Ephesians 4:26-27). When a demon attaches to a person it works to magnify the dysfunction in either the core personality or the sub-personality. If a sub-part was created that carries the emotion of fear, a demonic attachment will exaggerate the feeling of fear. Consequently, the person might experience terror or a full-blown panic instead of merely fear. If the person has a sexual issue, a demon might either make it obsessive or shut it down entirely. Demons will make sure that our behavior is not in the "normal" range.

As you read through the "catalog of symptoms" presented in this chapter you may suspect that we are developing a "theory of everything." While that is not necessarily our intention, Satan (an accomplished counterfeiter) and his forces mimic many diseases and afflictions. One reason spirits often go unrecognized is that they hide behind true illnesses. In Scripture Jesus would sometimes heal a person of epilepsy or cast out a demon. Sometimes Jesus healed those who were deaf and mute and other times He healed those with deaf and mute spirits. When demonic spirits work in concert with dissociation a myriad of symptoms can manifest.

Bear in mind that the things of Christ are foolishness to the world. Although the process we present will seem very simplistic to the sophisticated its effectiveness has been proved in literally thousands of cases. In the next few pages we will document the symptoms I have encountered most often in ministry and illustrate with stories of individuals who have been healed.

Insomnia, Sleepwalking, Night Terrors

A sub-personality will often have a different internal clock from the core, which produces an inability to sleep soundly. In many cases sub-parts were created in childhood as a response to situations that were very frightening, if not terrifying. In adulthood, the sub-part might cause the person to wake up in fear or terror as he or she emotionally relives that past experience. I recently prayed with a woman whose sub-personality stayed awake at night to keep watch and protect her. Her physical body was totally exhausted from sleep deprivation. Her insomnia resulted from a sub-personality who was "on guard" and would not allow her to sleep because she experienced trauma as a child when she was sleeping.

Demonic spirits can replay past hurts so vividly that that can actually seem like real-time experiences. Not only is the memory of events clear but the emotions are every bit as intense as they were when the abuse was "actually" occurring. A person will re-live the pain and agony, the fear and terror, exactly as it occurred in the past. One client would hear her parents' yelling every night many years after she had grown up and left the family home.

When reporting their symptoms to me, many clients list having vivid dreams or nightmares. I usually ask: "Have you ever tried to stop them through spiritual warfare?" I often get a quizzical look in

99

response because few people ever think to rebuke the enemy who is often behind such intrusions. Our culture has bought into the notion that dreams and nightmares are merely the creation of our own minds, but in most cases we can just rebuke the enemy afflicting us with such dreams and they will cease. This is especially true when our children are having nightmares when no major trauma has been experienced.

Another amazing though common result of rebuking a spirit in the morning is that in this way we can engage an internal protective response. After rebuking the enemy spirits in this way for four or five days, the dreams take on a very interesting defensive component. Very often the person will find himself actually rebuking spirits in his dreams! This rebuking is just as effective whether it is done the morning after the dream or days afterward.

Intrusive Thoughts or Imagery of Traumatic Events, Past Hurts, and Relationships

Because a sub-part seldom has the opportunity to release the hurt or pain, it is common for those who have suffered early traumas to constantly relive the experience. Take Nancy, for instance, whose mother was physically and emotionally abusive and had even prostituted Nancy for favors and treated her as a "throw away" child. It is hard to imagine that a mother could stoop so low. When tired of Nancy, the mother would simply leave her child in the care of other family members or even of strangers. Then, when she needed to use Nancy in one of her nefarious schemes, she would snatch her back for more abuse. As we prayed for Nancy, we discovered that she had created a sub-part filled with guilt and shame. Whether through some demonic machinations or her own coping attempts, a sub-personality was created that mimicked Nancy's mother. She continued to experience her mother's voice and appearance as an adult even after her mother had passed away. Nancy even went to the extreme of legally changing her name and appearance to distance herself from the memory of her mother…. Yet everywhere she went Nancy's mother was there, internally, tormenting her day and night. She could never escape. This demonic attachment was very acute. Nancy's unforgiveness, combined with the pain and hurt from the abuse, provided the enemy with powerful memories to repeat and emotions to crush her with depression and anger.

In other cases the opposite will occur, when, for instance, a person is in a treasured relationship that ends in a break-up. Say a couple is dating when they discover an incompatibility that necessitates a break-up. For one of the parties, however, an internal break-up does not occur. A sub-part may still be "in love" and unwilling to accept the end of the relationship. In such cases it becomes almost impossible for the core person to get "over" the breakup. This can occur with friendships for both children and adults. Tracy, for instance, had exactly this situation in one of her sub-parts that was enhanced by demonic attachment. When the enemy was oppressing her in this heightened state, Tracy was unable to function. She could not hold down a job or even perform basic personal care. Deeply depressed, she would curl up on the floor and sob for hours on end.

If the sub-personality surfaced during a sexual encounter, a demonic spirit would create a "soul tie" in the relationship to further intensify the attraction. The spirit would not let go until both the core and the sub-parts had confessed the sin and broken the "soul tie." If the enemy is involved in the relationship, the emotional attachment could be overwhelming and totally incapacitate the person.

Repeated Attraction to Abusive Situations

Have you ever noticed how common it is for a person who grew up with an unloving or abusive parent to wind up in relationships with the same type of abusive partner—over and over again? We shake our heads in consternation over the consistently bad choices certain people make in selecting a mate or even friends.

I have discovered in several persons I have worked with a sub-part that had a hope or dream of parental love. We all know when we are unloved. In some cases a sub-part is created that is looking for love. Because a parent is the desired source of love, the little child within tries in vain to get love from the distant parent. As the child progresses into adulthood she remains driven emotionally by the insatiable need for love. Because she wanted it from her mother or father, she will instinctively look for someone *just like the abusive or distant parent*. In fact she is actually attracted to the abusive person precisely because she wants to fix the previous dysfunctional relationship.

Spiritually the enemy loves this because he can provide all the irrational reasons to make these choices seem right. He can give a person a "feeling" of love or convince her that she can change the person or even cause her to overlook all the similar dysfunctions she had experienced with her parent(s).

Tracy had several inner children just like this. Through relationships with women Tracy was seeking the love she was never able to receive from her mother. Her father was "unsafe," emotionally and physically abusive. Although her mother was very loving, Tracy's Dissociative Identity Disorder (DID) prevented her from connecting with her mother's love and led her to suffer isolation and emotional abandonment. Her first gay relationship was with an older woman. She was really searching for another "mother" who would be there for her and not leave. She wanted to be safe from unsafe, abusive men.

Years ago when I was in Vietnam I had a good friend named Mike. I was not a Christian back then and had no spiritual insight. When I look back on that year now I can see the earmarks of spiritual manipulation. When Mike and I would go into Saigon for some free time or maybe to run an errand, an unusual occurrence would repeat itself. Mike was a "recreational" drug user. Every time we ventured into the city someone would approach him and try to sell him drugs. They never said a word to me. One day I asked him pointedly if he knew any of these people. He could not recall ever having met any of them. We finally let it drop, but I never forgot the confusion I felt. Why would they only approach Mike and never me? Now I see it as a spiritual attraction. Enemies hooked up in the spiritual realm and drew these drug pushers directly to Mike.

Just as Mike and the drug pushers were attracted, I have found that other victims and abusers are attracted. The enemy is able to spiritually orchestrate these connections.

Tracy experienced this in her gay relationships. A common term used in the homosexual community is the word "gaydar," and gays and lesbians pride themselves on being able to identify other homosexuals. This is accomplished with the aid of demonic spirits who make the identification.

Physical Symptoms with No Known Cause

Undiagnosed illnesses are a major symptom of dissociation. Although the sub-personality itself may not experience an actual illness, the enemy can mimic a wide variety of symptoms. The existence of a dissociative part affords the spiritual enemy a territory and legal right to remain for extended periods. This prolonged residence is often expressed in symptoms of physical disease.

I once prayed for a man who had a bleeding ulcer. Immediately after we removed the enemy and the attendant curse the issue of blood ceased. I have seen people delivered from seizures, dyslexia, stuttering, migraines, anorexia, bulimia, chronic fatigue, partial deafness, and a wide variety of diseases that were assumed to have a physiological cause. Again, please understand that I am *not* saying that all of these conditions are of demonic origin or byproducts of dissociative issues. What I am saying is that some of those I have counseled are immediately released from these afflictions. The parallel in Scripture is that we see instances in which Jesus would *heal* some persons of conditions such as epilepsy (a dis-ease of physiological origin) and *cast out demons* from others (a dis-ease of spiritual origin).

This raises the question: "How do you know which to do—pray for healing or cast out a demon?" The answer is: I do not know. In many cases there is simply no hard-and-fast way to distinguish one from the other. When in doubt I try both. Casting out a demon is typically the more immediate solution, and if a demon appears in relation to commands (i.e., spirit of epilepsy) I have a high level of suspicion that we might find a spiritual (demonic-related) cure. For this reason, during my initial interview I get a complete list of the person's physical symptoms and diseases. Just before I send the head demon to the foot of Jesus I run through the list and call up spirits associated with the afflictions and command the spirit to tell the person of his involvement in those areas. Then I cut off his assignments and ask the Lord to restore the person to the whole condition that He desires for him or her.

Chronic Suicidal Thoughts or Self-Injury

The enemy's ultimate intent is that we take our life. In John 10:10 the enemy (thief) came to "steal, kill and destroy." Although in Scripture we never see Satan taking a life, we do see him trying to entice Job and Jesus to commit suicide. In the book of Job, Satan tells God that his plan is to get Job to "curse God and die." Interestingly, just a few verses later Job's wife speaks the exact same words that Satan had spoken to God in Heaven. It does not take much imagination to speculate that Satan or one of his emissaries had suggested these words to Job's wife. When Satan was tempting Jesus in the wilderness he misquoted Scripture as a ploy to get Jesus to jump off the cliff.

In the book of Job some may argue that Satan killed Job's children. I have come to believe that may be merely a deception. Job never actually witnessed his children's death, which was merely reported by a messenger. The messengers were liars, obviously, for each one declared that he was the *only one* to escape. At the end of the story Job was blessed double for everything he had lost to Satan. But we note that only 10 children were listed, exactly the number Job allegedly lost and of the same gender: seven boys and three girls.

I have prayed with countless Christians who have entertained suicidal thoughts. Hundreds and hundreds have either plotted or attempted to commit suicide. In Scripture God alone is credited with the giving and taking of life (Deuteronomy 32:39-40). It is God who numbers our days. Satan is merely permitted to deceive us into taking our own life, which explains his attempted deception of Jesus and Job.

When I met Pat for the first time it was an "emergency." Although he was planning to take his life he was careful not to tell anyone his exact plan because he knew that doing so would get him admitted to a mental health facility. Pat was a drug abuser and had allowed some strong, difficult spirits into his life though his substance abuse. When I met Pat the enemy had gained so much strength that Pat could barely control his own body. He would be driving along when suddenly the thought came: "Run into that pole" or "drive into that parked car." He could not shake the temptation. As I prayed with him we discovered a young child inside who had been cursed with the words "I wish you had never been born." This little boy wanted to fulfill his mother's wish and just die. It was the little boy who had originally got Pat to rely on drugs to numb his hurt and self-disappointment. The day I met with him the enemy had taken the thought patterns and emotions to the final phase. It took several months for Pat to secure his freedom.

Periods of Amnesia or Gaps in Consciousness

By definition, dissociation implies that information will be held in a compartment that is separated from the core. Often as a dissociated part surfaces and contains the full memory of an event that the core personality is entirely unaware of. New information is revealed. God designed our minds with the amazing ability to shield the core from extreme trauma. Amnesia is quite often this exact condition. In amnesia victims the core personality was so traumatized that the memories were suppressed and even repressed out of memory and awareness.

Such was the case with Patricia, a woman who came to me for prayer and had great gaps in her adult memories. After a few weeks we discovered that Patricia was not her real name. In fact, Patricia was a 14-year-old part of a 24-year-old woman. The core had been so traumatized by satanic ritual that it had been suppressed for several years. Many years of Patricia's life were missing. A more accurate way to think of it is that years of Patricia's life had been "misfiled."

It is very common to find someone who experiences Obsessive Compulsive Disorder (OCD) to have dissociated parts that are the real culprits. For instance, Brian was a young man who had to repeatedly check and recheck his front door when leaving the house to see whether he had locked the door. In the creation of sub-personalities, Brian had a coping part that was tasked with ensuring his security (hence, the repeated security checks). Unfortunately, Brian had another sub-personality that was the primary automobile driver. As Brian would lock the front door and turn toward his car an internal shift would occur as the other part surfaced. These two parts were so deeply divided that information would not pass between them. As soon as the driving part surfaced the coping (security detail) part was suppressed and Brian could no longer "remember" whether the door was locked. Once the two parts were fused into the core, Brian no longer had a "memory" problem. The memory (e.g., whether the door was locked) was not lost but merely misfiled.

Memory gaps are very common in people who dissociate. In fact it is part of the protective process. Often a person will fear ministry to their part because they are terrified of what is hidden in the dark past. The fear is enemy-based because he wants his foothold to remain hidden. That memory gap might contain a legal right or stronghold that, if addressed, will forever release the person from bondage. No matter how much the person you are working with fears the ministry, you must coach him or her to allow the probe to continue. Their greatest fear is usually that the memory will impugn a loved one. The truth to share in coaching is this: "If you love the person at this time, regardless of the information discovered, you will just forgive your loved one and the relationship will heal."

Intense Shames, Guilt, or Feeling of Defilement

The enemy's primary tools include shame, condemnation, and guilt. If he succeeds in keeping us in this mental and emotional state our work in the kingdom will be severely stunted. Whenever I work with a person who feels he or she is unworthy (or perhaps even unable) to minister on behalf of Christ and no amount of confession seems to clear these feelings, I suspect that dissociation may be the culprit.

Angie came to me in this condition. As a young adult she had made the mistake of aborting her baby. She knew it was wrong, but family members and friends persuaded her that it would be "best" for her and the child, who would suffer if brought into this world to be raised by unmarried woman with few resources. When she came to me Angie was deeply wounded by her choice and unable to cope with her tragic mistake. Although Angie had confessed her sin daily for years, she felt progressively worse as the years passed. Dark depression and even thoughts of suicide haunted her daily. As we prayed with Angie and gained access and ministered to a dissociated part, she was finally able to experience freedom.

Demonic spirits wear two hats: They are involved in temptation, but once we have yielded to temptation and succumbed to sin they immediately swap hats and become the "accuser." Adding to the deception, accusations come in the first person so that we think they are our own thoughts: "I'm stupid." "I'm guilty." "I'm ashamed." These are the devastating thoughts that consume so many victims of demonic invasion. The dissociated part has no way to fend off deception and instead offers a "safe" haven for the enemy to operate.

Explosive or Uninhibited Anger

Alex was referred to me because his rage was so explosive that it had caused legal problems. Alex explained how when he got angry he would almost blackout. It was as though someone else came out in the rage. Alex could not explain why he would get so mad, many times over such minor things. "Why do I get so out of control?" he asked with tears welling in his eyes. As we worked with Alex it was pretty easy to trace his anger back to a time in his life when his dad had passed him over for his brother. His father picked his brother to play baseball with him even though Alex was the better athlete and wanted to play. His brother had no interest. Although it is likely that Alex's father was probably just trying help his less-athletic brother Alex was very hurt. As the little boy surfaced, the statement he made with tears was "it isn't fair!" So in adulthood whenever Alex encountered a situation when life was not fair this 7-year-old part would surface to express the pent-up hurt and the anger. By the time Alex was a young man the accumulated hurts that the 7-year-old boy was storing had become overpowering whenever he was faced with a triggering event of unfairness.

In a similar case Joel recalled an event that occurred when he was five years old. He was afraid to go down the slide in the park. His father coaxed him to give it a try and promised to catch him at the bottom. Joel was afraid to do it and made his dad promise over and over that he would catch him at the bottom. He finally mustered his courage and started down when his dad got distracted by Joel's sister. Unfortunately, his dad did not catch Joel as he had promised. Even though Joel survived and had no mishap at the bottom of the slide he was deeply wounded over his father's broken promise. As the years passed Joel encountered many situations in which family members or other trusted friends broke their promises. By the time Joel reached 13 his anger had become so intense that, when triggered, he was uncontrollable. His mother brought him to me because the staff at the private school he attended had decided to dismiss him because he was simply too dangerous to the other students. Once that 5-year-old boy was healed and had forgiven his father and others who had failed him, Joel was free. He was readmitted to the school and has had no further explosive outbursts of anger. He is beginning college this year.

Alterations in Major Belief System (Faith in God, Purpose in Life, Worldview)

So often in this ministry I hear people question their salvation. At times they feel totally secure and have a flawless confession of faith, but at other times they will feel distant and empty and wonder whether they are saved. They may feel unworthy or question whether they have committed the unforgiveable sin. The reason they feel so isolated, alone is that the Spirit is not present in that sub-part of their personality.

Many times I will pray with people who have parts that want to accept Christ. An especially powerful sermon might succeed in reaching into the depth of a dissociated person so that a sub-personality responds and prompts the Christian (i.e., the core personality) to come forward at the invitation. In rare times these sub-personalities might actually succeed in coming forward and confessing Jesus as their Savior. I recently worked with a young man who practically lived in church attending services and events four or five times a week. As I worked with him I found many sub-parts, all of whom had accepted Jesus Christ as Savior. Our session did not last long since all I had to do was to integrate the sub-parts. They did not know that they could integrate and wanted to know how their function would be handled in the core. After I explained that they would not disappear because God wanted them to continue to operate as they were—only in cooperation and unity with the core—the sub-parts were willing to fuse and integrate.

On a few occasions I have had dissociative converts who have come to Christ from various religious backgrounds. In these cases an interesting phenomenon can occur internally. Different sub-parts of the personality can accept different religious practices. Karen was very confused internally over different religious practices. She was divided between the doctrines of several different churches she attended. Internally, she might be divided between Pentecostal vs. Nazarene. When working with someone like this it is very helpful to be equipped as an apologist. Imagine for a moment that one part holds all the doctrines of one church and another part holds all the doctrines of another church!

Some time back a young lady named Allie was referred to me. She was diagnosed with Multiple Personality Disorder (today she would probably have the label Dissociative Identity Disorder) and was practicing both satanism and Christianity. When I asked her to tell me the basis of her salvation, Allie answered correctly. Her testimony of Jesus and His atoning death on the cross was clear evidence that Allie was a Christian. As we began to work with Allie, different parts began to surface. One was still a fully practicing satanist. Another part practiced new age cult worship. Obviously Allie's belief in God changed drastically when parts related to different religions would surface. Imagine how confusing Allie's life was. The treatment consisted of clearly sharing the Gospel with each sub-part and doing some apologetics work where required. Allie began to heal and come into internal spiritual agreement.

Extreme Confusion or Inability to Focus

Most dissociated persons have great difficulty in making decisions. Sub-personalities often disagree with the core regarding decisions that need to be made. Take a young lady named Sally, for example, whom several men had abused when she was a small child. A sub-part was created to store these memories and was quite justifiably terrified of men. As she approached young adulthood Sally desired to explore safe male relationships with the prospect of getting married and starting a family. Internally, however, she continued to feel threatened by men and at some point she would withdraw emotionally and bring the relationship to an end.

Those with multiple parts often speak of making a decision with "the committee" inside. More often a person will make a decision and then be in turmoil due to disagreement among the internal parts.

This confusion can carry over into marriage. Jennifer had been happily married for about a year. Her relationship with her husband Steve seemed quite normal except that, at times, she would feel very distant from him to the point that he seemed like a stranger to her. In praying with her we discovered that Jennifer had a suppressed part—a seven-year-old girl—that would surface occasionally in her emotions and had no idea that Jennifer was married to Steve. In fact, the little girl sub-personality was frightened of him and would cause Jennifer to withdraw from him.

The good news for Jennifer was that even though the little girl part had never made the decision for Steve and in fact did not want to because she was afraid of him, she was able to make the decision for Christ, which enabled us to reject the enemies. It took about 20 minutes for Jennifer to be able to choose her husband from within each sub-personality and then integrate with the core!

Severe Mood Swings

Given the nature of dissociated parts, severe mood swings are very common. As I mentioned earlier, in my experience three types of parts are often created in approximately the same time-frame. The first part created is usually a *soul pocket* that carries the memory of the event and has emotions such as fear, sadness, pain, or hurt. When a pain part surfaces a person may cry for long periods of time and suffer intolerable depression and even experience body memories of abusive treatment.

A second part often created also contains the memory of the abuse, but this one is enraged and angry rather than sad. When it surfaces the person boils over with these emotions. A good example of this kind of emotion is road rage. I have prayed many times with people whose road rage was the result of a part that would trigger in traffic not because of the immediate circumstance but rather in response to the injustice and rudeness of the other driver that causes the part to re-experience the earlier injustice or abuse.

A third part is commonly created for the purpose of controlling the emotions of the other two parts. I call it the *coping* part. This part usually has little or no emotion and is responsible for keeping the other two parts from surfacing at inappropriate times.

As these three types of parts rise up into the emotional level (Holly Hector's diagram) a person might experience periods of depression or fear (or both) and then suppress those emotions only to become angry or aggressive. In counseling I can see this cycle play out in the span of a few moments. After the two emotional parts express their frustration, a non-emotional protector will emerge, and the person will have experienced an emotional swing ranging from the lowest low to an angry high and end in an emotional flat-line condition. All this can happen in a matter of minutes. The depth of the emotion as each part emerges hinges on the depth of the hurt and the demonic attachment, if any.

Rick's close friend Robert brought him to me. Rick was suffering from deep depression and had been hospitalized for weeks. The moment Rick was discharged Robert whisked him to me for counseling and prayer. As we prayed, it was obvious that Rick had a spirit on him. As I began talking to him he grimaced and his facial expression was contorted. The most amazing thing about Rick was that of the hundreds of parts that had been created only one or two housed unforgiveness. The majority of the parts housed a stronghold of unbelief, fearing that he was not saved. My major task with Rick was to lead these small parts into a confession of Christ. Even before he had completed the confession his face would transform from twisted agony into peaceful bliss. As a part would surface the enemy would pounce. The moment that part was healed, however, the spirit would back off. In that respect Rick's experience was not unlike Tracy's.

Inability to Show Emotion (Love, Anger, Sadness)

I have been praying recently with a woman whose countenance and demeanor could be best described by the word "zombie." She would tell me, sometimes in great detail, of the horrific abuse she had suffered as a child. Although she was molested, beaten, raped, and threatened with death, she shared the entire experience in a stoic, matter-of-fact manner, with no emotions—no sadness and not a shred of anger. She spoke as coolly as if she had been sharing a grocery list with me.

I know from long experience that as I continue to pray with her at some point deep rage and pain will surface and demand to be dealt with. I suspect that I will not find one big part but many shards as though her soul were shattered like tempered glass. Many parts of anger and pain will emerge. We have already discovered the coping part whose name is "the protector." The protector was created to keep her from expressing any emotion. It had to be extremely strong because if those emotions leaked out when she was a child the severe consequence would have been even more devastating abuse.

The net effect on her life today is that she is unable to express any emotions. When she thinks about her lack of emotion it arouses some feelings of fear, shame, and guilt. She cannot understand why she feels that way.

In many women with similar abuse experiences we have discovered a *succubus* spirit. A common theme of this spirit is to defile sexual relationships. A succubus spirit will tempt the person to sexual relations outside of marriage and even wanton promiscuity, but as soon as a Christian couple is married his ploy is to shut the marriage down sexually. In men this spirit will be called an *incubus* spirit.

Loud Thoughts or Voices Inside or Outside of One's Head

About 15 years ago a pastor from a neighboring church called and asked if I had time come over and pray with a young man who was sitting out in their church parking lot. When I arrived I found Rob sitting on the ground wearing only one shoe. I never learned the fate of the missing shoe. Rob immediately knew that he was safe. I am not sure how he got that information, but it helped me to have his immediate trust.

One of the first questions Rob asked was, "Can demons be in cows?" He explained that he worked on a dairy farm and kept hearing voices come from the cows. They would beg Rob for release and implore him to cast them out of the cows. I explained to Rob that he was probably hearing demons that were following *him* and not the cows. Demons often deceive us about proper doctrine to cause confusion. You cannot imagine how many times I have heard that "the FBI is in the attic" or "something is in my ductwork" or "a voice is coming from my refrigerator." In every case it turns out that the voice is the enemy following the person.

Rob had two issues. First, demonic enemies had gotten a legal right in his life through drug abuse. Second, he had a part that was created because he felt unloved as a child. On the outside Rob would hear the screaming coming from the cows, but on the inside there was a little boy who would actually have compassion on the cows and demons and want them to be safe and loved. Rob could actually hear both of these voices and repeat every word they said. Over the next few weeks we were able to do inner healing and rid him of the source of both voices.

Unexplained Fluctuations in Creative and Intellectual Skills

This is especially apt to occur when a person's dissociation is high on the continuum line depicted earlier in Charles Kraft's analysis of "Trauma Induced Dissociations." These people might experience wide variations in life skills, functioning, or tasks. For example, one young lady had one part that was able to complete her college degree and another sub-personality with the vocabulary and life skills of a young child.

Different parts can be created to perform different work tasks such as homemaking or tending to the children. Each part becomes very skilled at the assigned task while having little or no ability in other life tasks. For instance, my co-author Tracy, though highly-skilled and well-trained in the legal profession, was terrified whenever she had to appear in front of a judge because a little girl part inside of her would emerge terrified of an authority figure's disapproval. Tracy would have to fight against the little girl's emergence or risk losing most of her ability to present her cases. Her little girl inside was traumatized and unable to function.

Isolation or Avoidance of Friends and Family

The extreme case of the demoniac of the Gerasenes (Mark 5) reveals a man who had isolated himself from society. He was living in the tombs. Not only was he isolated but he was cutting on himself and engaging in other self-destructive behaviors. Today we see many such men and women living on the streets. Although some of these people are hiding from the law, most are practicing extreme avoidance because of spiritual oppression.

A few months ago a young man named Gary came to the parking area of our counseling office, which is located in an office complex. Gary approached Tracy as she got out of her car. Tracy recognized Immediately that he was in spiritual bondage and invited him in to the office. As we talked with him, Gary admitted that he was on the run and had been drinking. We probed his history, but Gary could not explain exactly why he was isolated from his family. He just did not feel safe with them and suspected they were out to "get" him. When we asked if Gary was wanted by the police he said they were trying to find him. "Why?" we asked. Once again his answer was that his family was trying to "get" him. If we had done a background check we would have probably found no legal strikes. I contacted his one local family member, a sister, who reported no current issue other than Gary's irrational "fear." Gary's sister freely admitted that Gary had experienced many forms of abuse during his childhood. His mother and step-fathers had all been drug abusers with all the typical dysfunctions associated with addiction. Gary had experienced no care and no love and had suffered both physical and sexual abuse. The result was that Gary had created sub-parts to carry the abuse and they were all in the state of terror and shock from his abusive childhood.

Spiritually the enemy compounded Gary's fears with emotional terror and the fear that he was being singled out for punishment. We were unable to help Gary fully because like so many homeless people he became spooked and eventually disappeared. Though we were able to heal several parts that first day, he only came back one time. We tried to get him into a home and find support for him but, sadly, he just slipped away. Gary is like so many of the homeless people we have tried to help through our ministry. On a positive note, several have come free and are leading productive lives. We have been very effective with individuals sent from Zion Worship Center's homeless ministry because they have a very strong core ministry to support and care for these people.

Extreme Panic or Terror Cycles

Many years ago we were a referral ministry for Dr. Neil Anderson's "Freedom in Christ Ministries." One of our contacts received a call one weekend from a man named David. He was in a nearby motel and desperately wanted someone to come help him. David was in terror. When our ministry team arrived we found him curled up in the corner of the room whimpering like a little child, which in fact was exactly what had surfaced into his emotions. What we met that night was a terrified six-year-old little boy in the body of a 28-eight-year-old man. Picture it: a 6-foot-2-inch tall man with the tattooed physique of weight lifter and a booming voice. That was David. He was terrifying to behold, but at that moment in the motel room he was totally frozen in terror.

As we prayed with David it soon became clear that he had a traumatic experience of abandonment at age six. He described a terrifying argument with screaming and yelling and threats of harm. There was a physical altercation with pushing and shoving that ended when his dad stormed out in a rage. The experience terrified young David. As we worked with David we discovered that every time when he felt he was being abandoned this six-year-old part would surface. The current trigger that led us to him was a breakup with a girlfriend.

Cycles of Inappropriate Loss of Sexual Inhibitions

A very common occurrence among females with a history of sexual abuse is the creation of a sub-personality that has few or no sexual inhibitions. Imagine how a little girl who experiences ritual sexual abuse copes with it? For many, the coping mechanism involves creating a sub-part of herself to experience the abuse, which leaves the rest of the core unscathed by the unwanted and defiling abuse and memories of it. The memories of such horrific experiences are sometimes completely repressed and only surface as the parts are healed.

Alice was an satanic ritual abuse (SRA)survivor. As we began unraveling her internal system we discovered a little girl whose function was to provide sexual release for other members of the cult. When Alice finally broke free of the cult and actually escaped to another state, she found herself succumbing freely to men's sexual advances. This occurred because the little girl in her, who was created by the cult for precisely that purpose of responding freely to satisfy others' sexual desires, would surface when men began to show her attention. Alice was baffled over why she was unable to resist the advances even of men whom she found unattractive. The reason was that a succubus enemy was attached to the little girl sub-part and its purpose was to attract men to Alice. It seemed the enemy was able to selectively introduce unsafe men into her life. Sadly, Alice was not able to enjoy any healthy male relationships.

A former pastor named Thomas came to me for help with a sexual addiction. It had ruined both his marriage and his church ministry and he was still struggling with strong temptation. He explained how whenever he became attracted to a woman she would seem immediately attracted to him. Within a few weeks, however, the affair would run its course and Thomas would lose interest in the woman and was subject to temptation by another woman. His thoughts were constantly bombarded with sexual images and memories. Thomas had given up on confession and breaking soul ties and was growing weary of attempts at deliverance. Nothing had brought him to a place of peace.

As I worked with Thomas we were able to locate several sub-parts created by incidents of sexual experimentation in his childhood. During his youth he and his close friends, both male and female, had explored pornography and other sexual stimuli. Through these events Thomas picked up both succubus and incubus spirits. These demons lay dormant for many years, but as Thomas matured they began to manifest in his life, especially when the little parts would trigger up into his emotions.

These demonic spirits worked to connect Thomas with women who were damaged as he was or had similar spiritual tempters. Until we were able to heal the inner parts the demons were able to control much of Thomas' sexual life. In his case the enemy worked to expose his sexual sin as well. In other words, demon spirits want not only to be successful in their work of temptation, they also want the person to be exposed so that they can wreak the most damage in the person's life— hence, Thomas' ministry was ruined when his sin was exposed. An example of this exposing work is that a lying spirit will suggest new lies that contradict previous lies so that the person is exposed as a deceiver.

Years ago I learned about the slumber party game "Bloody Mary." Neil Anderson lists the "game" in the *Steps to Freedom* as one of the occult experiences to confess and renounce. The game is often played by young women who invoke a spirit with a chant that I will not repeat here. The ritual is typically performed in bathrooms with lit candles, and as the girls call on this spirit they will often see a spiritual entity appear in the mirror. This game invokes two spirits. The first is an incubus spirit and the second is a spirit of Molech (the god of child sacrifice). I have found at least a 90% correlation between this game and young women having abortions. The succubus spirit attracts the girl into sexual relationships and fornication; then, when she becomes pregnant the Molech Spirit tempts her to abort the child.

In praying with women who had played this game and later aborted a baby I have found that they seem to have no ability to "say no" to male suitors and the option of abortion was always discussed as a means of birth control. As we lead these women to freedom we confess the sexual sin to break soul ties and then identify and confess it as a sacrifice to Molech. This final confession seems to cause a physical release for many women who have played "Bloody Mary."

In praying with gay men and women I have always found a succubus or incubus spirit. With Tracy the succubus demon directed much of her emotional life. In women who struggle with same-sex attraction the main culprit is the succubus spirit. In men the succubus spirit will drive them to obsessive sexual addiction. In men who experience same-sex attraction the offending enemy spirit is the incubus, which causes male-to-male attraction. A woman who has an incubus spirit will often experience a sexual presence assaulting them in nightmares and dreams. If the person has a traumatized sub-personality these spirits cause obsessive behavior as the primary stronghold. Incubus and succubus spirits attempt to defile all sexual relations beginning with same-sex attraction. These enemies will tempt an unmarried heterosexual couple to engage in fornication. If the couple later marry the enemy will then shut down the sexual attraction. A common report I hear is that a couple seemed to have great sexual relations until they got married. After the wedding one of the partners lost interest in sex.

Checking Out with Drugs, Alcohol, Unreasonable Eating Behaviors, or Exhaustion

As we discovered earlier, the typical order of part creation is that the first one takes the pain. The second part manifests the anger, rage, or frustration. The third part is usually a coping part created to distract or overshadow both the emotional pain of the first part and the anger components of the second part.

Since coping parts are influenced by demons the coping mechanisms tend to be dysfunctional behavior. Common coping behaviors include fatigue and eating disorders but may extend to more destructive behaviors such as drugs, alcohol abuse, or sexual dysfunction.

Over the past few years I have been assisting several local church ministries with their recovery programs. A common theme among those participants who cannot sustain their victory is a coping part that is the culprit. Sometimes the person manages to suppress the coping parts for years only to have some minor trigger surface the part and immediately lead the person to succumb to temptation. The sub-parts have no will power to withstand temptation. In fact, they were created for just the opposite—to literally run to the problem and engage in the dysfunctional behavior to "cope" with the pain parts with their feelings of sadness and anger.

Betty was a recovering alcoholic. As we prayed with her we discovered both a pain part and a coping part. Throughout her life Betty had been abandoned over and over. In young adulthood she turned to alcohol as the escape—as a constant companion and means of coping with all the emotions stirred by abandonment. As we began to trace Betty's history of relapse we found that it was always precipitated by the loss of a boyfriend, a cherished friend, or even the death of a loved one. These "loss" events in Betty's life triggered intense and prolonged pain and her only relief was the anesthetic of alcohol. In Betty's case it was not just a little alcohol on occasion because her coping part surfaced for extended periods, which led to prolonged binges.

When she first came to see me Melissa was overweight. As a child she was sexually abused. The abuse began in her pre-teen years and continued until she was 16. Over these years she developed a coping part that protected her by overeating. Melissa had no idea that her obesity was a sequel to the abuse she suffered as a child. The sub-personality's objective was to ensure that Melissa remained overweight so that no one would want her because the weight was a barrier that would keep her safe from the sexual attention.

Periods of Behavior in which there is Reversion to a Childlike State

The literature dealing with the "inner child" concept is vast. Often in counseling a client will share that he feels like a little kid. This is often related to issues with authority figures.

Randy shared that every time he was around his father he would begin to act like a little child. He was intimidated by his dad and agreed with behavior and statements that were so unlike his "normal" personality. As we prayed with Randy we immediately probed for a little boy who was looking for his dad's approval. In just a few moments it surfaced and gave a testimony that explained his unusual behavior with his dad. His father was quite authoritarian in shaping Randy's thinking. If Randy did not agree he was disciplined or sometimes just whacked. Randy thus learned to fear that anything he said would incur a punitive repercussion. A part was created to store some of his father's aberrant behavior, and this terrorized little boy inside would never buck his father's opinions regardless how unreasonable they might be.

Often when I pray with someone a sub-personality will fully surface and the person will turn into a child right before my eyes. Although this may have never occurred in the person's life, the potential has always been there. Almost every person with Dissociative Identity Disorder (DID) I pray with has these "little children" trapped inside. It is common that a created part will never grow beyond the age when the abuse first occurred. I want to be clear that this phenomenon is a part of the deception. The sub-personality is really not a child but is exactly the same age as the adult. Their life skills, however, may be limited to what they have experienced during the times they have surfaced. If I encounter a part that may be too young to speak, I ask the Lord to grow the sub-personality up so that it can think and act like an adult and communicate as an adult. Immediately, the part will begin to share his or her story.

False Spiritual Empowerment

On numerous occasions I have discovered false religious parts. In some cases they were created in relation to cults the person may have explored or been exposed to as a child. More often, however, the parts are created to replace God. I have found parts named "God, "Father," "Holy Spirit," and "Jesus." These parts will attempt to lead the person spiritually. What makes them very convincing is that they may offer spiritual "help." Sometimes an antichrist spirit with unholy spiritual gifting is associated with these parts. Like a psychic with a familiar spirit the person is constantly sorting through spiritual input he believes is coming directly from God. In most such cases the part's "Christianity" will be extremely distorted with legalism. They will often have extensive scriptural knowledge but usually with a legalistic twist.

Chuck was exposed to a satanic ritual during his stay in a medical institution. He already had damage and many sub-parts created through childhood sexual experiences. When the ritual was performed an antichrist spirit attached to some of these damaged sub-parts and morphed a few of them into a full array of deity parts. As our team (I was assisted with two other partners) counseled Chuck he would go into a trance-like state and speak to us as though through a direct word from God. It was a very unsettling experience for our team because the words were so spiritually powerful. After a while, however, we were able to discern that it was not the Lord speaking. Using the binding and testing techniques described in the chapter "Dealing with Demons" we were able to locate and heal those sub-personalities and shut down the antichrist spirits.

Chuck had been shattered as a child and visualized *thousands* of sub-parts inside. He had not only false deity parts but also waves of soul pockets with a host of confused and false doctrines. Our work with Chuck involved bringing the deity personalities to Christ and asking them to work as protectors. For weeks we would ask the sub-parts to present their questions. Every time we met was like a theology class. During the last half hour of each session we would bring forward a host of sub-parts, and most evenings hundreds of them would be fused.

Teresa came to me after pursuing relief from intense spiritual manifestations for several years. Though she had a strong Christian leaning from childhood her mother had been an occultist. As Teresa grew up she was drawn away from her mother's spiritual choices. As an adult, she accepted Christ and became very involved in church. She sincerely loved the Lord and was always available to serve in various ministries. As she matured, her spiritual quest led her to a large charismatic church. During a special service at that church Teresa received a special "anointing" from a pastor. Once endowed with the "gift" she was able to "slay in the spirit" and call out demons. Her ministry was in full bloom until one day she gave a prophecy and later learned that it did not come true. When she made the declaration out loud to her husband, immediately the enemy came out of the closet and tossed her to the ground. She experienced demonic voices in prayer sessions, her body would quiver and quake, and she could not get a full night's sleep. The condition progressively worsened, which sent Teresa on a two-year pursuit of deliverance that finally ended at our counseling ministry.

As we prayed with Teresa we discovered that her sub-parts had actually taken on traits of demonic spirits. They would hiss at me and talk in a guttural, demonic-sounding voice, and not surprisingly some things they said did not ring true. One "demon" part assumed a protective mode over another voice. Demons rarely protect one another. I conducted a few tests and was able to determine that the voices were not demons but sub-personalities. Over a period of time these sub-parts were healed.

Once the sub-parts were healed I called the demonic spirit that empowered Teresa to "slay in the spirit" and she slumped in the loveseat "slain." In Teresa's case the spirit was false. We needed to confess her participation in occult practices, renounce her false empowerment, and reject the spirit that deceived her.

As I mentioned earlier, demonic spirits mimic God's spirit. They parody God's true gifting. We see this principle clearly in the beginning of *Steps to Victory* (moriahfreedomministry.com). In Teresa's case the spirit was false. Granted I have only had three cases of it but I am yet to come across a true gifting of "slaying in the spirit." As with many "gifts," I do not see any advantage in trying to make a judgment whether "slaying in the spirit" is a valid gift. My approach is simply to test the spirit.

Emotional Reversals

Dissociative parts will often experience *emotional reversals*. I observed this symptom for the first time several years after I became involved in this ministry. Terri was a troubled young teenager whose home life was in turmoil. Her father had abandoned the family, her mother was an alcoholic, and at the tender age of 14 Terri was essentially on her own. Terri shared that she felt dirty, ashamed, and defiled. As she shared the details of her situation I noticed a series of cutting scars on her arm. When I asked why she did that Terri explained that it hurt until she cut but that once the incision was made the pain released. I thought I had misheard her, but she repeated the experience again.

Since that day I have encountered numerous cases of cutting, which is typically a combination of a dissociated part and a demonic spirit. One of the spirits will respond to the name of Baal. In the Old Testament Baal was invoked by cutting. We see an example of this in the confrontation between the Prophets of Baal and Elisha.

> "It came about at noon, that Elijah mocked them and said, 'Call out with a loud voice, for he is a god; either he is occupied or gone aside, or is on a journey, or perhaps he is asleep and needs to be awakened.' So they cried with a loud voice and cut themselves according to their custom with swords and lances until the blood gushed out on them." (1 Kings 18:27-28)

The dissociative part will typically carry a spirit of guilt and shame.

What is important to note here is that Terri's emotions were reversed. What she felt was exactly the opposite of what she should have felt. She felt pain until she cut, but once the incision was made the pain would subside. When the sub-part was released from the demonic influence her emotions returned to normal and Terri stopped her cutting behavior.

Mandy experienced same-sex attraction similar to my co-author Tracy. But Mandy had a number of other symptoms that originally brought her to the counseling ministry—depression, grief, and sadness. Mandy also experienced some minor demonic manifestations that caused her to investigate a spiritual solution. Many of her symptoms were familial. Several members of her family both ancestral and current were either presently involved or had been involved in same-sex attraction. Depression was also a common theme. As we prayed with Mandy we discovered that she had been damaged in the womb, for an ancestral sexual spirit had inserted itself into her life soon after conception. Mandy had a "flipside."

For Mandy the statement "I was born this way" was in part true. God had not intended her to be gay, but a succubus spirit had come down through the legal rights established and unconfessed in previous generations. By the time Mandy emerged from the womb the ancestral spirit had gained a strong "flipside" fortress. As Mandy grew of age she was always attracted to women. Even though she knew it was not right, she simply could not change the way she felt. As I

121

counseled with Mandy a core stumbling point was that, although she had faith that she could be delivered from depression, fear, anger, and substance addiction, she found it exceedingly difficult to imagine being delivered from same-sex attraction because that was simply "who she was."

As we prayed with Mandy we found a "flipside" and led it to Christ. A few other issues that needed inner healing were resolved and then we removed the head demon whose main functional assignment was sexual distortion. Mandy is no longer attracted to women. It was the demon's emotions driving the same-sex attraction—not hers. She immediately became attracted to men and could not even imagine why she had felt same-sex attraction.

Chapter 5: Tracy's Spiritual Search

Tracy: In our first meeting, Jim presented the "bubble theory" and helped me to understand the principles and symptoms of dissociation. I readily identified with the concepts he presented and could sense the sub-parts surfacing into my emotions as we finally acknowledged them.

Jim: I asked Tracy to tell me about her spiritual journey. I was looking for spiritual entrances. Such entrances can be anything from participation in other religions to unusual Christian experiences, especially those related to charismatic practices such as prophecies, dreams, visions, tongues, etc. These entrances can either be curses or lead me in a direction for healing.

Tracy: When I accepted Jesus as my Savior as a child, I knew the decision was the right one but I also wanted Jesus to heal my pain inside. By the fourth grade I was aware of the deep void in my heart that longed to be filled with the love of a mother who would care for me and not abandon me. I lived without God during most of my childhood and adolescence. I struggled as a Christian in college but wanted desperately to walk hand-in-hand with God. I tried to read His Word and occasionally attended church, but I did not trust or believe that the Lord loved me enough to heal my pain. I was defective and He knew it … and was not loving enough to fix it.

I arrived at this place of turmoil from a lifestyle of same-sex attraction, dysfunctional and abusive experiences, and deep emotional pain. Though by the time I reached college I had already been in Christian therapy for many years I was still drawn to the gay community in hopes of having a satisfying relationship and being loved—having that void in my heart filled by a woman who would love me and not abandon me. I lived in a gay community for nine years and participated in the gay lifestyle.

I was attending Christian therapy twice a week the whole time because I wanted to be whole and healed and I wanted God. I knew that I was living a double life, but I was a prisoner to my emotions, thought-life, and identity. The therapy concentrated on issues of dealing with daily life because I was so injured that I did not know how to make decisions about basic everyday issues and as a result the therapist, in essence, had to re-parent me.

I would start each session in pain, often crying. My therapist would speak to the adult or the emotionally surfaced part and get the pain to subside. I would leave composed (in my core personality), but within a few days normal life experiences would easily trigger the sub-parts carrying all the pain and confusion and I would struggle to survive until my next therapy session. Later, when I began working with Jim I learned that my therapists were ministering not to the hurts deep within me but rather were treating the symptoms without addressing the source of the pain.

My relationships with women always ended due to internal dissonance and turmoil: I was a Christian and I wanted a family but desired a relationship in which I would be loved deeply and securely by a woman. A male relationship was unsafe, so I chose to pursue women for comfort. I was attempting to duplicate a normal family life and tried hard to rationalize living in a same- sex relationship, especially since the climate toward homosexuals was drastically changing. However, I could not.

I was sinning intentionally and angry at God for *making me the way I was* even though all the while Jesus was telling me He was there. He pursued me, connected Himself to me, and deep down I knew that living as a gay woman was not an option.

When I was 29 years old a significant event occurred that gave me hope. I asked God if "He was real." I went to bed that evening and had a dream from the Lord. The angel that I believe God assigned to watch over me, my guardian angel, took me on a journey. We walked through a cemetery on a path, and only the path was lighted. Throughout my walk on the lighted path evil and black pressed in from both sides. The angel took me to a dusty room filled with old books. He picked up a book, blew off the dust, opened it, and began to read. I immediately knew it was God's Word. The words lifted up off the pages like a wave of words and went straight into my heart quenching a deep spiritual thirst. I was stunned because this was the first time that the Word entered my heart and was not dry. I woke up the next morning and cried out, "You *are* real!"

I knew this was my angel and God was showing me that I was to walk out my healing. There would be darkness and the enemy would press in to stop me, but the Lord showed me in the dream that His Word would be like soothing streams and that I would be successful because I would walk with Him.

On account of this dream and many other experiences from God, I could not be a borderline Christian, yet internally I had always felt He was distant. I was committed to finding the truth and wanted a personal relationship with God. I believe that He gave me a character of tenacity that would stop at nothing until I found the truth—*no matter what.*

After my dream the Lord started doing small miracles, giving me more dreams, visions, and personal moments with Him. I believe that He was beginning to prepare me to do spiritual warfare. I first experienced freedom through spiritual warfare when a friend and I casually read some prayers in Neil Anderson's book *Steps to Freedom*. Months later I realized that I was no longer hearing voices. As a child I used to hear voices calling out my name over and over in a mocking, demeaning tone. I was always afraid to sleep because the voices usually came at bedtime.

I attended a Christmas service at the Vineyard Christian Fellowship in Malibu. A guest pastor gifted in deliverance spoke and prepared the audience for a time of healing. I was the first person Tim called to the front, and he told me that the Lord said I was in "torment." That word that the Lord gave Tim was the exact emotion I had been living with for months. Tim touched me and the power of God moved through me like electricity, starting at my head and going down toward my feet and I fell. Tim touched me again and again I felt God's healing power moving in me. At that moment He gave me a picture in my mind. I saw God take a curved needle like a sewing needle with thread attached to it and pierce one side of my heart. He took the needle across a tear—a wound—and pierced the other side and then pulled the suture taut so that it closed the tear in my heart. I immediately knew that only God could heal the torment. Since that night I have never experienced this same level of torment, even though I continued to feel deep pain and other debilitating emotions for some time. This was a powerful experience that helped me to understand deliverance and know that God loved me.

I began attending the Vineyard Church in Malibu. During one service the pastor's son, Grant, touched me, rebuked an "assignment" over my life, and my body felt electrified. Grant told me that the Lord revealed to him that I had an assignment of depression over my life. Up until that day I had been taking anti-depressants for most of my young adult life. From that day forward I never picked up another pill. Through this the Lord again showed me His power over darkness and His authority over the enemy.

Jim: Tracy had three significant audible "God" events in her life leading to ultimate healing. Eventually all of these were to play an important role in securing her freedom.

Tracy: During my first year in law school the woman I was dating came to visit me one evening. As she walked up the stairs to my apartment, opened the door, and stuck her head in, I heard God speak in an audible voice that filled the room, but the woman was unable to hear it. God told me: "She's the last." Even though this woman should have heard God's voice, she did not. I alone heard it.

As soon as God said this, I knew that He wanted me out of the gay lifestyle. Although it took a while to walk fully out, I knew that He said, "It's over." Within six months I moved out of the community I had lived in for six years and relocated to Malibu and attended Vineyard Christian Fellowship.

A few weeks later as I was worshipping during an evening church service I looked up at one of the worship band members and once again God spoke audibly. His voice filled the church, yet no one else heard Him. The Lord said, *"You could love him."* Immediately I felt my heart expand and fill with love for this man. I walked around with an enlarged heart of love for three weeks. This was so important to me because for the very first time I felt love for a man.

Jim: This second Word Tracy received gave her hope. The previous statement was initially a burden because she knew she that God was calling her to quit her lifestyle, but at the time Tracy did not know how she was going to be free of a lifestyle both physically and emotionally. For Tracy the first Word from God was a command. The second revelation was God bringing His mercy. He had given her the direction, now He was proclaiming that she would change from the inside. As she moved in the direction God wanted her to go she would be accompanied with the power of transformation. Tracy could do it because God would change her emotions and empower her to obey.

Tracy: The Lord was not done speaking to me audibly. A few months after that church experience, I was walking through my parent's kitchen on my way to law class when God's voice filled the room. He said, "You don't trust Me because you don't know Me." I knew that the Lord was encouraging me to seek Him and not to quit—*no matter what.*

Based upon these three audible sayings, I lived my life looking for a cure for the internal pain and turmoil. I was unable to live with the status quo. God began to give me personal miracles, always guiding me toward the next step. I began to understand spiritual battle and worked hard at obtaining spiritual deliverance from abandonment, rejection, and other demonic attacks.

Although I was experiencing more freedom than I had ever had, I could not help the constant feeling of young, immature, and very painful emotions that would never leave and from which I had only occasional and momentary respite. Women would also consistently enter my life and trigger up the sub-part, Clarissa, and I would again find myself involved in a same-sex relationship. (I would learn later that Clarissa was the name of a three-year-old sub-personality who was desperately seeking love.)

I could not understand what was happening and simply assumed this was "normal" living. I was getting older. Families were growing up. And there I was stuck—still in no man's land longing to love and fall in love, and yet I could not because I couldn't be with a woman long-term and was unable even to go on a date with a man.

Although God had begun to prepare me for the concept of dissociation, in the summer of 2008 I didn't realize that this was a major key to my healing. The first time Clarissa surfaced, it was a young girl in pain. Other sub-parts, each having a name and age, were also created based on the trauma I experienced. Somehow on a subconscious level I internally dissociated, which afforded me a form of protection and coping whenever I experienced childhood trauma. The first 10–15 sub-parts were very significant, and most of the gay issue was contained in Clarissa.

In January 2009, having tried over the preceding 15 years to do everything I knew to heal, I felt that no one could help me. I was on the brink of giving up and losing all hope. From my teen years on I had asked God to heal me, to take away the pain, to bring a man whom I could love into my life, to have the ability to read His Word, to align me with His will, and to make me normal. Nothing had worked and nothing was working.

On a whim I Googled the words "deliverance + Orange County" and up came a Web site for Moriah Ministry that spoke of deliverance and had a testimony of a woman's own healing journey with Jim Hanley. Since I lived 20 minutes from Moriah Ministry, I drove to the church that very day and met Jim. That January night my life began to change. Weekly Jim and I counseled, and I began to understand the concepts of dissociation, sub-parts, the core, inner healing, and deliverance. Although I cried during my first counseling session with Jim, it was during our third session together when we recognized that it was a sub-part surfacing who was later revealed to us as Clarissa. This is when the inner healing began.

Jim: After talking with Tracy for just a short time I could see "Clarissa" on her countenance. It took several more weeks to gain her trust and actually begin the healing process.

When I first begin to counsel with a new person I am in the lookout for the signs of internal response. I noted how Tracy's face began to change and assumed the look of a hurt child. As she shared her story her eyes teared up and her voice became a tentative whisper. I could imagine that she was reliving part of her childhood right before my eyes.

Chapter 6: Tearing Down Fortresses

In this section I will present a diagram adapted from Neil Anderson's book *The Bondage Breaker*. I have modified it in two ways. First, I have omitted the surrounding flesh because we are concentrating specifically on the soul and, second, I have removed the dividing lines between the mind, will, and emotions because in my experience people do not seem to compartmentalize their souls in this way. When a person dissociates, the soul pockets will seem to have all three components. This truth is especially obvious in those suffering from Multiple Personality Disorder (MPD). Each personality will have a mind, will, and emotions.

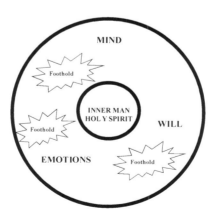

Figure 4: Undamaged Soul[31]

When we accept Christ, the Holy Spirit is injected into the center of our being. His identity is perfect within us. When we have footholds they exist in our old soulish, fleshly, carnal nature. As we grow in Christian maturity the Spirit fills us. In the Bible, being filled with the Spirit is related more to our obedience than to having a spiritual experience. Singing "fill us with your Spirit" may make us feel good but we should not expect it to be effective so long as we are still walking in disobedience. As we examine the diagram, we see that footholds need to be removed. These are erased as we confess our sin and forgive those against whom we have harbored bitterness.

This diagram helps us to understand the battle that Paul was waging as he described it in Romans 7. He was at war against his old nature.[32] As he was trying desperately to grow his "inner man," he records sin as having its way within him. The battle that Paul was waging was the will of the "new man" vs. the will of the "old man." In another place Paul talks about having the mind of Christ.[33] Paul was waging a mental war on the battlefield of the mind. That is the mental front of the two natures. John wrote about letting "His [Christ'] joy make our joy complete." That is the emotional front of these two natures. We are to allow the Holy Spirit to fill us, pressing out the old nature and being filled with the new. The process is summarized in confession and obedience.

Many who come to Christ are able to begin a victorious journey immediately. They seem to grow with no major spiritual hindrances. All is onward and upward. Others, however, come to Christ and the battle begins. They seem to get body slammed and dragged into a spiritual battle that is overwhelming. They try everything to make it stop. They stop at nothing in trying to experience the spiritual victory that others believers seem to enjoy. They read books, listen to CDs, attend seminars, and seek spiritual guidance, but despite it all they always fall short. Before long they are discouraged and defeated.

Instead of enjoying a relatively undamaged inner soul like that shown in Figure 4, they may suffer from trauma-induced dissociation as shown in the Figure 5. The internal walls created to protect the core personality from these damaged areas seem all but impenetrable like the walls of a fortress.

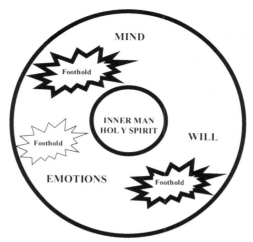

Figure 5: Trauma-Induced Damage

The footholds (fortresses) in Figure 4 are strongholds of different world views and sins. In other words, they are the lies we believe. Now let's consider the extreme case depicted in Figure 5. These fortresses or strongholds can be so strong that they do not even know God. They have no knowledge of Him. How can this occur? As we discussed previously, parts can be created within us that are locked in time. Parts created before a person has accepted Christ are independent of the core and have a totally separate identity. The extreme example (Figure 1) I presented in a previous chapter depicted someone diagnosed with MPD (Multiple Personality Disorder), but fortresses do not have to be that extreme. Sometimes they are subtle and well hidden. In all cases, if they are created before the person (core personality) accepts Christ, they may carry no knowledge of Jesus.

I know it may seem strange that a person can be "in Christ" and still have an aspect or part of the soul that is unaware of Him. An illustration might help. Imagine that we are like a house. Our house may contain many rooms. As we tour the house we can go freely into most of the rooms, but the doors to several of the rooms are closed, even locked. They are inaccessible. When we apply this analogy to ourselves we see that we can have areas of our lives that are totally exposed and open to the indwelling of the Holy Spirit whereas a few areas can be walled off. These are the extreme cases of fortresses. They are not merely ideas and imaginations that are not in agreement with God but literal strongholds within our soul that do not even know God.

Theologically we are not saying that these people are "not saved." In fact most are very sincere Christians who serve actively in many areas of ministry, some even on staff at many of our churches. Though they can lead full, rewarding, and effective ministries, inside they know that something is just "not right."

An Old Testament Analogy

Let's couple Paul's statement in 2 Corinthians 10:3-5 with an Old Testament analogy to help us understand this condition. The New Testament launches us into the comparisons.

> "For I do not want you to be unaware, brethren, that our fathers were all under the cloud and all passed through the sea; and all were baptized into Moses in the cloud and in the sea; and all ate the same spiritual food; and all drank the same spiritual drink, for they were drinking from a spiritual rock which followed them; and the rock was Christ." (1 Corinthians 10:1-4)

Throughout the New Testament the writers use Old Testament examples to teach New Testament spiritual truths. In this passage Paul used the story of Israel's deliverance from Egypt under Moses to illustrate our own Christian journey. Paul used this New Testament phenomenon called "typology" more than any other New Testament writer. There are some excellent books on typology and even dictionaries of typology. The word "typology" comes from a passage in Hebrews chapter 11 where Paul was presenting the heroes of faith.

> "By faith Abraham, when he was tested, offered up Isaac, and he who had received the promises was offering up his only begotten son; it was he to whom it was said, 'IN ISAAC YOUR DESCENDANTS SHALL BE CALLED' [translators emphasis]. He considered that God is able to raise people even from the dead, from which he also received him back as a type." (Hebrews 11:17-19)

Note the very last word in the quote—type—from which we get the title "typology."In this passage Paul tells us that Abraham's offering of Isaac is a "type" of God, the Father's offering of His only

132

Son Jesus. Just as Abraham received his son back, God the Father would also receive back His Son. The interesting thing about typology is that once the door is opened to the Old Testament stories we note that the characters continue to fulfill their role. Abraham becomes a "type" of God the Father in this passage. Isaac subsequently is a type of Christ in his marriage to Rebecca (a type of the church, the bride of Christ) and his servant represents the Holy Spirit.

Throughout the New Testament these "types" help us understand spiritual truths. In Galatians, for instance, Paul uses Abraham's marriage to his two wives Hagar and Sarah as types or symbols of God's first covenant with the nation Israel and His second covenant with us Christians. In the passage 1 Corinthians 10:1-4 above, Paul was saying that the rock that Moses struck in the wilderness was a type of Christ. The meaning that Paul was conveying was that just as Moses was to strike the rock once and living water was drawn out, Christ was to be struck down once (i.e., on the cross) and would become our living water. Moses' critical mistake was striking the rock the second time.

As a "type" of Christ the rock was supposed to be spoken to—*not struck*—for all subsequent needs. Likewise, Jesus was to be struck *once* for all of us. Thereafter it was necessary for us only to speak to Him to receive the living water. The penalty for Moses' angry outburst—not being permitted to enter the Promised Land—might seem excessive. But if God had not demonstrated how serious Moses' error was, He would have communicated the wrong message. What's more, His response also demonstrates another doctrine of God. The law (Moses) cannot carry us into the Promised Land. Instead, we must instead follow Yeshua into the Promised Land. The Hebrew word Yeshua in the Old Testament was translated Joshua, which in the New Testament is Jesus. Just as the children of Israel could not follow the Law (Moses)—but only Joshua—into the Promised Land, so in the New Covenant we cannot work our way into Heaven but must follow Jesus to the promised eternal life with God.

Yet another type of Christ is the Ark of the Covenant. I will present it here because we will use this imagery a bit later. The Ark contained the unbroken tablets of Moses, just as Jesus kept the law and was sinless and carried in Himself the law unbroken. Also inside the Ark was the re-budded rod of Aaron, which represents life out of death. Jesus would come alive after his death on the cross. The Ark also contained the jar of manna, with which God nourished the

Israelites on their journey to the Promised Land. Jesus said, "I am the true manna who has descended from heaven."

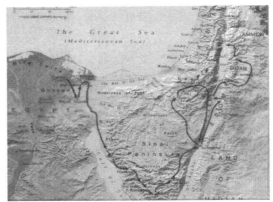

Figure 6: Deliverance from Egypt

With a preliminary understanding of typology, let us follow through the symbolism that Paul is creating in 1 Corinthians 10:1. Paul says that they were "baptized into Moses in the Red sea."

> "For I do not want you to be unaware, brethren, that our fathers were all under the cloud and all passed through the sea … and all were baptized into Moses in the cloud and in the sea." (1 Corinthians 10:1-2)

Paul was using this typology comparing our spiritual journey with the exodus from Egypt. Just as Moses and the Israelites were escaping from bondage in Egypt, so we also are escaping bondage from sin when we repent. When we turn away from sin we are essentially walking away from its bondage. In 1 Corinthians 10, Paul refers to this act as being baptized into Moses. Baptism means to be "immersed in," but spiritually it more nearly means "to come into fellowship or agreement with." Because Moses was the lawgiver, he represents how following the law removes us from the bondage of sin. This is not unlike a person in AA (Alcoholics Anonymous) or NA (Narcotics Anonymous) who is trying to overcome the temptation to abuse alcohol or narcotics. They will repent from their behavior and join a group to help them be accountable in withstanding further temptation (i.e., breaking the law). So as the Israelite's journeyed out of bondage in Egypt into the Sinai Peninsula by following Moses and entered the Promised Land by following Joshua (which means "deliverer"), so we believers escape from the bondage of sin by following Jesus our Deliverer (through faith).

Wandering in the Wilderness

Although there is a great benefit in escaping from the bondages of sin, the escape or exodus itself only brings us into a state of wandering. There is no rest and no peace. We must then wage battles and struggle constantly with the rigors of life. Often the person who escapes from bondage desires, like some of the Israelites, to want to go back to the familiar bondage (i.e., Egypt). There is a tendency to want to go back to a life of sin and all the captivity that it entails. In our previous example of the person in AA or NA, the Sinai Peninsula is symbolic of a life without Christ, a life of wandering without rest and peace, a life of trying to "white knuckle" one's freedom. The truth is that it is just a short step away from captivity.

As they wandered in the Sinai Peninsula the Israelites feared actually entering the Promised Land because of the giants there. Those giants are types that represent the battles we Christians face. The doubts, the restricted life, and the mockery that Christians often experience are the giants we have to face. And we, too, are sometimes tempted to want to go back into Egypt because the former enslaved sin-life often looks better than a life of wandering.

Entering the Promised Land

In order to find rest, a home, and a place of settled life, one must make the next step. In the example we are exploring, this means that we must be willing through faith to follow Jesus into the Promised Land. Moses, who represents the law, cannot lead us into the Promised Land. We must enter by faith in (the willingness to follow) our leader is Yeshua. It is the land of "milk and honey." It is the place where God promised the Israelites that they would find rest. It is a place of blessings in lieu of curses.

In Acts 2:38 we see that there are two steps in becoming a Christian. After understanding the Gospel we must first repent. Repentance is turning away from our trust in something or someone (often ourselves) other than Jesus Christ for our salvation. The second step is to trust in Jesus. We must confess Him as our Lord and Savior. In the story of Israel two events symbolize this process: leaving Egypt and crossing the Red Sea symbolizes repentance turning away from the bondage of Egypt and the false security of Pharaoh; following the law (Moses) and then following Joshua and crossing the Jordan symbolizes confession of Jesus.

Finding Rest

Having entered the Promised Land one might suspect that all is well on the way to *happily ever after*. We have entered a place of peaceful existence and life is now an experience of "milk and honey." This is a false expectation, however. When a person becomes a Christian and enters into relationship with Jesus, it is the beginning of a new life. It is not an easy life. This world is full of tribulation and temptations, and in order to have a fulfilling and rewarding life we must learn how to live as Christ leads us. In the Promised Land there are new battles to be fought. Just as Joshua faced perils in the land of Canaan, so we believers must fight our own battles. Our assignment is the same as Joshua's—to take possession of the land, clear out the enemy, and occupy the territory.

As the story of Joshua unfolds we see that the Israelites had to carry out precisely this assignment. The Israelites faced three types of battles or deceptions. Each one symbolized a type of struggle that we must face in our Christian walk.

I even believe that they are given to us in the order in which we need to address them to achieve our freedom and victory in Christian life. I am going to reverse the order here, however, because the focus in this chapter is on the first battle. Since I do want you to see an overview of the entire process, I will start with the *deception of the Gibeonites*, followed by *the sin of Ai*, and then we will examine the defeat of Jericho, which I believe clearly typifies the process of defeating fortresses or, in secular terminology, healing dissociation.

The Deception of the Gibeonites

God gave the Israelites strict orders that upon entering the Promised Land they were to destroy the inhabitants of the land and enter into no covenant with them. After the Gibeonites learned that the Israelite "invaders" had destroyed both Jericho and Ai, they decided to try a little subterfuge in order to keep the Israelites from destroying them. Joshua chapter 9 records their ploy, a successful deception that would cost the Israelites dearly over many years.

"But when the inhabitants of Gibeon heard what Joshua had done to Jericho and Ai, they worked craftily, and went and pretended to be ambassadors. And they took old sacks on their donkeys, old wineskins torn and mended, old and patched sandals on their feet, and old garments on themselves; and all the bread of their provision was dry and moldy. And they went to Joshua, to the camp at Gilgal, and said to him and to the men of Israel, 'We have come from a far country; now therefore, make a covenant with us.'" (Joshua 9:3-6)

The Gibeonite deception represents the covenants we make with the world, the compromises we make with worldly idols. Scripture also identifies them as strongholds. As I am writing this chapter this very day, the Episcopal Church appointed a gay bishop in Los Angeles. Though the church is called to be tolerant and supportive of sinners who are attempting to overcome their sins, we are not to be tolerant or supportive of those practicing sin and making no attempt to overcome it—or, in some cases, even redefining the sin as *not* sin! The principle is taught clearly in 1 Corinthians 5. Paul describes another sexual sin in which a young man was sexually involved with his father's wife. Paul's response was to turn the young man over to Satan for his unbiblical behavior. Homosexuality is labeled a sin and as such should not be advocated as a lifestyle, much less deemed behavior becoming of a leader in the church. Though in our day it is politically correct to be gay or tolerant of the gay lifestyle this is nothing less than a compromise with the world that is a Gibeonite deception. We have changed our views; God has *not* changed His views. Our world is seeking political correctness, but sometimes to be politically correct is to be biblically wrong. If we fail to recognize homosexuality or any other transgression as sin, we fail to acknowledge the truth that there are consequences from God. Freedom from bondage comes only through confession—both in the core personality and in the sub-personalities—and will not come when we deny sin.

Make no mistake: I am not against gays. If I were I would not be in such close friendship with my co-author and her friends, who are my friends, too. My point is that as long as a Christian practices a gay lifestyle, although his salvation may not be in doubt, his freedom will not be secure. This is equally true of Christians who abuse drugs, who have sexual relations outside of marriage, or embrace any other sinful practice. Please do not jump to the conclusion that I am saying that gay persons need to "white knuckle" their freedom, either. That is not what I am saying. With proper guidance, inner healing, and deliverance, that person can be filled with the Holy Spirit who will bring and internal change in those old desires. The road to freedom is not denial of God's truth; rather, God's truth is the *only* way out of bondage.

A few years ago a missionary family who was serving the Maasai in Kenya returned on furlough. They would typically spend six months in the United States and then return to the wilds of Africa. America had become so unsafe, and its media so morally decadent, that they felt it was far safer to take their children back to Kenya. This is evidence that we are seeing the Gibeonite deception working its way through our culture as we compromise ever more carelessly with worldly values.

The Sin of Ai

The second battle we must wage as new and maturing Christians is to discern, confess, and renounce the behaviors, sins, and practices that God has told us to avoid. The following story of Achan's sin illustrates this high-stakes battle.

> "But the sons of Israel acted unfaithfully in regard to the things under the ban, for Achan, the son of Carmi, the son of Zabdi, the son of Zerah, from the tribe of Judah, took some of the things under the ban, therefore the anger of the LORD burned against the sons of Israel." (Joshua 6:1)

What Achan did was to appropriate something that God had directly told the Israelites to avoid. Achan was disobedient in taking the idol. Achan's sin can be likened to any sin that we Christians refuse to stop committing. We see a parallel in the New Testament as believers renounced their former occult practices and removed all occult books and associated paraphernalia.

> "Many also of those who had believed kept coming, confessing and disclosing their practices. And many of those who practiced magic brought their books together and began burning them in the sight of everyone; and they counted up the price of them and

found it fifty thousand pieces of silver. So the word of the Lord was growing mightily and prevailing." (Acts 19:18-20)

We can see this principle in the Old Testament in many forms. In the book of Joshua we see the practice applied in Ai. Achan had taken something that was under God's ban, and the Israelites could not be victorious until the transgression was radically (meaning "from the root") removed, rooted out.

> "Israel has sinned, and they have also transgressed My covenant which I commanded them. And they have even taken some of the things under the ban and have both stolen and deceived. Moreover, they have also put them among their own things." (Joshua 6:11)

Likewise, each of us must root out any practices in our own lives that are under God's ban. In my ministry I use a thorough inventory tool such as Neil Anderson's "Steps to Freedom" with a few extra prayers and confessions to guide believers to confess and repent of their sins. Another great experience is an "Encounter God" weekend. Both of these experiences can bring a great amount of freedom to participants. As the book of Joshua unfolds we see this principle yet again at Mount Ebal.

> "Just as Moses the servant of the LORD had commanded the sons of Israel, as it is written in the book of the law of Moses, an altar of uncut stones on which no man had wielded an iron tool; and they offered burnt offerings on it to the LORD, and sacrificed peace offerings. He wrote there on the stones a copy of the law of Moses, which he had written, in the presence of the sons of Israel. All Israel with their elders and officers and their judges were standing on both sides of the ark before the Levitical priests who carried the ark of the covenant of the LORD, the stranger as well as the native. Half of them stood in front of Mount Gerizim and half of them in front of Mount Ebal, just as Moses the servant of the LORD had given command at first to bless the people of

Israel. Then afterward he read all the words of the law, the blessing and the curse, according to all that is written in the book of the law. There was not a word of all that Moses had commanded which Joshua did not read before all the assembly of Israel with the women and the little ones and the strangers who were living among them." (Joshua 8:31-35)

Mount Ebal represents the old nature where curses abound because our sins have entangled us. Mount Gerizim represents where God wants us to be—walking in His blessings. The problem is that by nature and practice we are sinners and often find ourselves on Mount Ebal. God has given two provisions in the typological picture that enable us to escape from Ebal. First, we have an altar on Mount Ebal where we can offer a sacrifice for our sins and thereby become free of the sins that entangle us in the curses. Second, we have the Ark of the Covenant that represents Jesus Christ who will allow us to bridge the gap to Mount Gerizim. When we Christians confess our sins Jesus transports us back onto the mount of blessing. In order to appropriate the blessings, however, we must proclaim them.

The Battle of Jericho

The third area of battle is really the first one a person must face to gain victory. It is the battle of faith and is symbolized by the battle of Jericho. When we accept Jesus Christ as our Lord and Savior the Holy Spirit seals us and enters our life and fills those areas we permit Him to. Unfortunately we might have fortresses in our lives that keep the Holy Spirit at bay. Obviously the question is not whether the Spirit has the power to take control of those areas—He does—but whether we will submit those areas to Him. When there is dissociation as we discussed earlier there might be walls within that are barriers to the filling process. In the book of Joshua the first battle that had to be waged was against the fortress of Jericho. Not only must the enemy be defeated but the fortress walls must be torn down. As long as the walls stand, there can be no permanent victory against this foe.

As Joshua led Israel into the Promised Land his first act was to send spies into Jericho.

"And Joshua the son of Nun sent out of Shittim two men to spy secretly, saying, Go view the land, even

Jericho. And they went, and came into an harlot's house, named Rahab, and lodged there." (Joshua 2:1)

The two spies then entered the city of Jericho. They were led miraculously to the home of a prostitute who had heard of Israel's victories in the wilderness wanderings. We are not told how the men found Rahab's home, but what's important to note is that because they followed Joshua's instructions they found themselves sequestered safely in her home.

Another thing to note is that Rahab made a confession of faith. She not only recognized Israel's military might but went one step further and acknowledged the spiritual empowerment behind their success. She confessed the God of heaven whom she identified with the God of Israel.

> "When we heard it, our hearts melted and no courage remained in any man any longer because of you; for the LORD your God, He is God in heaven above and on earth beneath." (Joshua 2:11)

The spies then directed Rahab to tie a scarlet thread in the window of her home to secure protection for herself and her family against the invading army of Israel.

> "Unless, when we come into the land, you tie this cord of scarlet thread in the window through which you let us down, and gather to yourself into the house your father and your mother and your brothers and all your father's household." (Joshua 2:18)

At this point in the story the spies retreated into the camp of the Israelites. Then God instructed them to march around the walls of the city with the Ark of the Covenant. When they did so, quite miraculously, the walls came tumbling down and the city was quickly defeated. The focus in this battle was taking down the walls.

This part of Joshua's assignment in the Promised Land is analogous to our assignment to tear down the fortress walls in our lives. When ministering to one whose fortress walls are as the city of Jericho, it is necessary to penetrate the area. Following Joshua's lead we send in spies, who in this case are counselors. Our objective is to find the "measure of faith," which in Joshua's story was Rahab.

> "For through the grace given to me I say to everyone among you not to think more highly of himself than he ought to think; but to think so as to have sound judgment, as God has allotted to each a measure of faith." (Romans 12:3)

Paul tells us in Romans that each of us has an allotment of faith. Paul made the statement in the context of telling us that each person in the body of Christ was endowed with a gift. I believe this truth can be extended to our physical bodies as well. If a person has been divided into sub-personalities, alters, or dissociated parts, each of these parts will have a measure of faith. Our objective is to activate the faith within these parts or fortresses.

The easiest way to achieve perfect consistency is merely to evangelize. In other words, gain access to and share Christ with the part. At this point you will apply pure apologetic concepts in the argument. It is no different from sharing Christ with a non-Christian except for the fact that I know that the part will eventually receive the Holy Spirit. Unlike a non-Christian, whom I cannot be certain the Holy Spirit will draw to Christ, sub-personalities of Christians (i.e., the core personality) will accept Jesus because He will finish "what He has started." Since the Holy Spirit is already in the core, all parts will eventually align with Christ. It is important in some cases to make a clear presentation of the Gospel and then wait. It is the Holy Spirit's job to lead to an understanding of truth. It is important that we do our part and then back away so that God can do His part.

Theologically, I do not believe that when I share Christ and the parts receive Him the Holy Spirit will then descend from heaven and seal this sub-personality for the first time. Rather, the person is already eternally sealed in Christ, which has already been verified. Accordingly I view this person as a Christian who is not completely filled with the Spirit.

Recall the prior analogy that likened Christians to a house with many rooms. The Holy Spirit may have been invited into the main part of the house (i.e., the living room or a family room) but has not yet yet gained access to some back bedrooms whose doors are closed or even locked. I see this type of "evangelism" more as standing at the "fortress" door and knocking on behalf of Jesus.

I can summarize the process of praying for a person with a "fortress" as:

(1) Make contact with the part.
(2) "Evangelize" the sub-personality(ies). At the very least I will lead him or her through a confession of Christ.
(3) I let the sub-personality tell the story of when and why it was created.
(4) I have the part forgive abusers and perpetrators.
(5) I lead the personality into a confession of sin.
(6) I have the part give up his or her roles in the core's life (i.e., sadness, depression, fear, shame, guilt, etc.).
(7) I then have the part confess any sexual sin and break any soul-ties if appropriate.
(8) Finally, I ask the part if he or she is willing to integrate with the core. At this point the work is sufficiently complete that God will take the part and put it back in the original place that God intended. I ask the core if he or she is willing to allow that little child back into the core. If the answer is "yes" then I continue by praying for the unity to be completed.

I usually offer a prayer like this: "Lord, will You take this little child and place him or her back into the core where he or she belongs. Lord, please make this man or woman into the person You envisioned before time began." At that point if the work is complete God will place the part back into the core. If it does not happen, it might be necessary to revisit one or more of the steps until the fusion is accomplished. The counselor can usually find any area of resistance to resolve simply by questioning the part and the core.

Just as the walls came tumbling down in the Jericho analogy, so the Holy Spirit can take occupancy of walled-off parts of a believer's personality. My final prayer is that the Spirit will fill any area within the person that the enemy has vacated. To conclude the inner healing after all fusion and integration is complete, I take the person through the *Steps to Victory* (moriahfreedomministry.com) to sweep the house clean.

James L. Hanley & C. Tracy Kayser

Part III: Tearing Down Fortress Walls

James L. Hanley & C. Tracy Kayser

Chapter 1: The Healing Path

In this chapter I will provide you with an overview of "the healing path" process, the typical sequence of steps I follow when working with a deliverance ministry candidate. See this chapter as a roadmap (or, to bring the metaphor into the technological age: a GPS) of deliverance ministry territory. From the initial interview and laying the groundwork for healing (through proper diagnosis and prayer) to effecting integration, this chapter is a guidebook. You will want to refer to it often, perhaps even reviewing it before beginning to minister to any new candidate for delivery.

The Interview

When I first meet with a deliverance candidate, I start by interviewing the person. I ask for a list of symptoms as well as why he thinks there is a spiritual problem. If he has come to me the problem is not merely physical or emotional pain. Something has caused the person to suspect that the symptoms have a spiritual source. If during the interview I hear one or more of the symptoms of dissociation I continue the interview by probing in that direction.

After probing for symptoms, I typically try to find out about any childhood traumas. (Current relationships are not relevant aside from providing me with a better understanding of symptoms.) If dissociation is present, the cause will trace back to something early in childhood. I am looking for rejection, abandonment, experiences of

147

fear, verbal or physical abuse, molestation, or anything else that might damage a young child. My objective at this point is to learn the ages that dissociation may have occurred because it will be helpful in addressing inner parts.

Another important area to discuss is the person's spiritual journey and what he has explored or participated in during his life. This might uncover the source of some spiritual components shared in the symptoms. Dissociation by itself will cause some debilitation, but if an enemy is introduced due to occult practices the symptoms can be magnified greatly and take on more ominous characteristics.

The preparation for ministering to someone experiencing dissociation begins with biblical teaching and providing an explanation for their symptoms that is not based in psychological terminology. This biblical truth is ultimately the weapon that will terminate the legal rights that the person has permitted and which result in demon attack. It will bring down the strongholds and show the right path to restoration. I usually start by sharing common dissociative symptoms but find that it is not fully received until I share an explanation from Scripture. For example, when I share the analogy from Scripture that compares our walk out of bondage with the Exodus story, a connection is made. This is exactly what happened is Tracy's case.

Share the Process and Theology

To present the scriptural basis for the ministry I typically begin with a PowerPoint slide presentation that summarizes the process and theology presented in the chapter "Tearing Down Fortresses." At some point during this presentation I will ask the person I am working with to describe the basis of his or her salvation. The right answer, of course, is for them to tell me about Jesus. If they begin to tell me about themselves then I know that we need to begin with a clear presentation of the Gospel. It is surprising just how many people have come to see me for help after years of ministry and counseling who have not asked Christ to be their Savior.

At this time I also address any doubts they have about their faith and let them ask theological questions. We may need to address the distortions concerning Christian demonization and doctrines that we examined (and debunked) in a previous chapter. It is imperative at the outset to strengthen the person's faith in Christ and the process ahead. It is almost impossible to do the kind of inner healing we are describing without full spiritual cooperation of the deliverance candidate.

Prayer

Notice that I have not yet mentioned prayer. I pray over the room and the situation before the person arrives, but I wait until *after the presentation* to bind spirits because they will trigger responses that help me discern the nature of the attack and how to proceed. I look for those reactions that may be triggered in two ways: (1) The words I say may bring the sub-personalities to surface because demonic spirits are the triggering mechanisms. (2) Another response I see during presentations is that child parts may surface with memories of hurts or sometimes with hope as they see and hear someone who finally "understands." Either condition helps me gain immediate access to the internal system of parts.

This is when I begin in prayer. The first thing I pray is to ask Jesus to join us to Him in the ministry to set His child free. I usually address Him as Jesus of Nazareth, the One who came in the flesh or the One born of a virgin. I might claim promises such as "He came to set the captives free" or that He came to "bind up the brokenhearted."

Then I move to the head demon of highest authority and bind him for the purpose of inner healing and to prevent interference. Over 90% of the time the head demon will carry the formal name of the person as recorded on his or her birth certificate.[34] When you think about this tactic, it makes sense that the enemy would like to replace the person. After all, he wants to fully occupy and control the person as his victim. In the prayer, I bind to the head demon his entire network and every spirit that reports to the head demon. In addition I bind up the gatekeeper. I usually say something like: "I bind up the head demon of highest authority (sometimes using the formal name on the person's birth certificate). I bind up the entire network reporting to the head demon. I also bind the gatekeeper spirits and shut down their ability to allow spirits into or out of the system. All spirits addressed are now bound, gagged, and rendered inoperative."

The above approach addresses the demonic forces as a military-like organization. What we see both in Scripture and in practice is that the demonic realm seems to operate through an organizational hierarchy. In the book of Daniel there is a prince of Persia and a prince of Grecia, which are dark angels. Angels that appeared to Daniel were fighting against them and were withstood for 21 days (Daniel 10:20). God's angels are sometimes arrayed in military ranks as well (2 Kings 6:17).

As I continue to pray I ask for guidance and gifting from the Lord before closing with a prayer of protection: "I forbid any manifestations or acts of vengeance or violence against any of our families, friends, or churches, in Jesus' name."

Probing for Sub-Personalities

After completing these initial steps I explain that I will begin probing for sub-personalities. I am looking for information about the part's initial creation because this will reveal the legal right. I am also looking for the part's role or function in surfacing in the core's life. This will expose the strongholds. I then need to discover why the part has not accepted Christ, which will suggest the apologetic argument I need to present. It is easier to tear down strongholds and allow for integration if the Holy Spirit has access to the part because the Spirit is the One who affirms the truth.

I tell the client that one of four things might occur:

(1) *The person might receive thoughts that are coming from a part in response to my questions.* If there is a part it will typically say something such as "I'm not here" or "leave me alone." These parts were usually created in situations of abuse and only surface to take more ill-treatment. They usually fear that they will face new levels of abuse.

(2) *Emotions may begin to surface.* They may feel rage, guilt, shame, fear or sadness. The emotions will be in a controllable range because the enemy is bound. Most often I will see tears forming in their eyes.

(3) *God will show them a picture or a memory of themselves at an earlier age.* This is usually a part being revealed.

(4) *A little girl or little boy shifts to the front of the person's psyche* and all of a sudden we are talking to a childlike part. (This fourth possibility is much more common than one might expect.) The core shifts to the background but does not usually lose total consciousness. Instead, the core is aware of everything that transpires and can even interact at different times.

I suggest that people close their eyes to help them concentrate on what might be going on inside. I explain that I will be speaking past them to parts of them deep inside (i.e., dissociative identities deep in their souls). I tell them they cannot do anything wrong except not tell me what they are thinking, feeling, or seeing in their mind.

Once I explain the process and what the person should expect, we are ready to begin. I have the person close her eyes and I begin to speak to her as I would to a young child or youth. If I suspect that there is a "protector" part I begin as follows:

> "If there is a protector for Amy, I want to commend you on the good job that you have done in Amy's life. We are not here to judge you because you have not done anything wrong. We know that you are totally exhausted. You have been carrying an enormous burden for Amy, but now that Amy has accepted Jesus Christ, Jesus wants to take that burden from you. He went to the cross to be our protector and to carry our griefs and sorrows, and He wants you to enter into His rest.[35] As a protector I know that it is your job to protect the internal system. Would you be willing to talk to me?"

As parts reveal themselves, we will need to interact with them according to the injury. I usually ask three types of questions:

(1) The first will be related to what caused them come into existence.
(2) The second question relates to what they do in the core's life.
(3) The third question relates to what is keeping them from accepting Christ with the core

When I ask these questions I ask the person to monitor what he/she is thinking.

In the process of identifying sub-personalities I typically start with an age that a person may have been traumatized. If the person's parents were divorced, for instance, I might ask if there is a "4-year-old girl who was hurt by her parents divorce?" I use the initial interview to pinpoint possible times (or time-frames) when the person may have been hurt and probe those events to find "soul pockets." As we uncover sub-personalities they will sometimes carry identities of the major demons that torment them. This is especially true of "flipside" personalities (discussed in the next chapter). Common names include those such as "outcast," "alone," or "despair." Many times the parts will have formal names such as "Trace" or "Clarissa." I'm not sure where these names come from. Protectors probably name them for their own use.

Clients can respond in four different ways to my questions. (1) If they are receiving thoughts in their mind I continue to address their thoughts in normal conversation to find answers to the above questions. (2) If they respond emotionally, I will address the emotion and the person's core seems to know exactly how to answer. (3) The third way is when a client has a memory or vision. I will question the part and the core will know the answer and relate the information to me. (4) The fourth way is when a part shifts to the surface and the process is just like talking to a child or a person whose age is the same as the surfaced part's age.

Inner Healing

As I minister to the protector, I can usually get a response. Some protectors, however, are very stubborn and it may take a few meetings to finally build enough trust. Once the protector is cooperative I explain that he needs Jesus in his life to accomplish his function because, although he may be able to protect the person physically, he cannot stand against the spiritual enemy. I might quote Matthew 12 that a "divided house will not stand" or that God issued only one set of armor. For protectors to be totally armored up they need to give their responsibility to Jesus so that God will find them a new purpose in the core.

Once I get the protector convinced that we have the right solution, the first step is to lead him or her into a confession of Christ. Theologically I do not believe that the Holy Spirit is sealing this person for the first time. Rather, I see it as though the Spirit already resides in the "house" but is now being invited to come into the "back bedroom." By inviting the Holy Spirit into this soul pocket I find that the person more readily receives the truth and healing can begin.

As I conclude the interview, I usually ask the protector to continue doing his job until we get all the parts under protection, into

Christ, and healed. I assure the protector that God will allow him to continue his job until all the sub-parts are healed and fused, at which time the protector can follow them into the core. This prevents the person from being in an unstable condition if we do not completely finish the work in the session.

The first step is to ask the protector for permission to talk to the person's other parts so that I may begin to minister to them, to heal them, and integrate them into the core. Once I get the protector's permission, I can then go to the next step. For each soul part identified, the remaining steps are the same as with the protector.

The second step is to let them tell their story. It is very important that these parts be given the opportunity to share. In many cases the core will have shared the experience over and over again in traditional counseling, but these sub-parts may have never been given a chance to express themselves.

The third step is to forgive the abuser, the perpetrator, and any people who should have protected the child. This step is very important because forgiving will stop the cycle of memories and pain. At this point the enemy will often surface, many times in subtle ways. If the person says "I can't forgive" or seems unable to speak words of forgiveness, I remove the spirit of anger or rage and thereafter find that the person will sail through the declarations. In fact, this step is so vitally important that I have included a separate chapter on forgiving.

The fourth step is to give Jesus the emotions and memories and break the strongholds. I direct the part to declare the spiritual truth that trumps the temporal truth. When Tracy's parts were at this stage, a common stronghold was "I am all alone and it will never change." These stubborn anti-truthful thoughts dredge up the hurtful memories and emotions. To break that stronghold I had Tracy declare the following spiritual truth: "Jesus will not forsake me. He will not abandon me. I have a spiritual family and I am not alone." At this point, although the declaration itself does not satisfy the need for physical presence it shuts the enemy down and produces a dramatic shift in Tracy's emotions as the overwhelming emotions are dissipated. This process actually involves giving Jesus the emotions instead of having Tracy bear the burden of her hurts and grief. Often overlooked is that just as Jesus died for our sins on the cross, He also died to bear our griefs and sorrows.

"Surely our griefs He Himself bore, and our sorrows

He carried." (Isaiah 53:4)

Once that step is complete the part can fuse and integrate back into the core. I ask both the core and the part for permission to bring about the integration. My prayer for this step may follow this pattern:

> "Lord, I ask that you would take this part and allow it to go back into the core where he or she belongs. Tear down the walls and barriers and allow this part to become one with the core. I pray that You, Lord, will make this man or woman into the person You envisioned from the very beginning of time."

Usually the person will experience some form of confirmation. For instance, he or she may feel something or God may show him or her a vision.

I repeat this process with each part until all the parts are fused. If at the end of the process I address the enemy he will finally surface. If the enemy does not surface I bind him and say something such as, "The soul part that the enemy was just hiding behind can come forward so that we can kick that coward out." Another part will usually surface at that point. Until the person is totally integrated, the enemy might surface but will not leave permanently. In most cases he will just hunker down behind the unfused part(s) because they are his fortresses. Until the last sub-personality is fused with the core, the enemy still has access to the person through any unfused parts because legal rights remain within those parts. The enemy is as strong with one part or many. Until integration is complete the enemy's strength, including all his emotional exaggerations, is not diminished significantly.

Soul Ties

My objective in dealing with any sub-personalities is to try to get them into the core as quickly as possible, which accomplishes a great deal for the person. From the core we can deal with all the issues and memories and give them directly to Jesus. Integration can occur before all sin issues have been dealt with the exception of those sins that the enemy has taken as a legal right. Normally legal rights are major sins associated with the initial trauma. One issue that seems to hold up the process of integration is "soul ties." The term "soul tie" is a term that describes a spiritual union between two people outside of marriage.

> "Or do you not know that the one who joins himself to a prostitute is one body with her? For He says, 'THE TWO SHALL BECOME ONE FLESH.'" 1 Corinthians 6:16)

When two people have sexual union they become united to one another. I believe that God has allowed this to occur for our spiritual unity. His intent is that we would be one in spirit and soul just as Jesus and the Father are one as Jesus declared in John 17. This actually works to the advantage of a married couple because one partner can "stand in the gap" for the other person's transgression. We see this principle in the book of Exodus. The Scripture records that Moses had failed to circumcise his son and as a result God was going to take Moses' life. Somehow Moses' wife Zipporah understood the transgression and stood in the gap for her husband.

> "Now it came about at the lodging place on the way that the LORD met him and sought to put him to death. Then Zipporah took a flint and cut off her son's foreskin and threw it at Moses' feet, and she said, 'You are indeed a bridegroom of blood to me.' So He let him alone...." (Exodus 4:24-26)

God honored Zipporah's act on behalf of her husband as we see in the final verse—God let him alone.

The problem with this God-given unity, however, is that it may also work against us. This is the problem that Paul was referring to in 1 Corinthians 6. This passage tells us that if a man lies with a prostitute he becomes one with her. In the spiritual realm we have labeled this condition a soul tie. Because the two are tied (e.g., marriage partners), if one spouse has an unconfessed sin that has brought an enemy into play, that enemy has legal access to both parties.

Under Mosaic Law divorce was permissible because of the hardness of our hearts. A man could issue a certificate of divorce to his wife. The certificate was an open declaration, both temporal and spiritual, that a soul tie was broken. In effect it stated: We are no longer "one flesh."

The problem Paul referred to occurs only when relations have been entered into out of wedlock. A tie is created in which we become one with the other person through sexual union. Unlike a broken marriage in which a certificate of divorce is issued, which breaks the spiritual and legal bonds, these ties established with unwed parties remain in effect. This gives the enemy all the right he needs to cross over and afflict the former sexual partner. For example, if a married man has an extramarital affair (and is the one walking in sin) his wife (who has remained faithful) can experience the same demonic intrusion as her husband.

How do we break the tie? It is very simple. We confess the sin along with any other covenants that we may have made. Then we make an out loud spiritual declaration: "I break the soul tie with _____ in Jesus' name" (fill in the name of the sexual partner). This declaration issues an open and notorious notice to the spiritual realm that there is no longer a spiritual oneness between the two partners. They are no longer "one flesh." I have a person do this for each sexual contact he or she has had outside the bonds of marriage. I have the person include same-sex relationships and even sexual activity that may have occurred with animals.

Chapter 2: Exceptions to an Inner Child Dissociation

There are three other areas or types of soul damage that can be frequently encountered in dealing with inner healing. The first is a flipside. The second is when the core has been "put to death." And the third is an interject. All of these manifest in different ways from a typical "inner child." More importantly each of these are identified and discovered in a unique way.

Flipside

About 10 years ago I was privileged to be in a week-long training session with Dr. Joe Albright. After a period of instruction and demonstration, Dr. Albright insisted that I do several sessions with him as a mentor. During one of our sessions we encountered a "flipside." After Dr. Albright taught us about the concept of a flipside we were then able to do the inner healing and integrate it into the core.[36]

Two related concepts are related to flipsides. The first is the concept of an ancestral spirit assuming the identity of the person's formal birth certificate name. The second concept, which is at least as (if not more) important, has to do with splitting of the soul. Although I had encountered flipsides in ministry before the training with Dr. Albright, I had not understood exactly what I was experiencing. Other deliverance ministries had encountered the phenomenon and had just classified it as another sub-part. After the training session with Dr.

Albright, however, I had a clearer understanding of what I was dealing with, which made it much easier to find the path to healing and integration. Over the past 10 years I have verified this information in my own experience with countless clients.

I had encountered flipsides in ministry, but had never put a label on the condition. In the early nineties I had attended a seminar on Satanic Ritual Abuse (SRA) and one of the topics of discussion was this concept of a divided soul. Many of the victims of SRA , they had discovered, had a split in their being. At the time they had used the Ying and Yang symbol to describe it, with a dark side and light side. At that time I was uncomfortable with the concept especially as they linked it with an eastern philosophy. Yet in ministry I found that the condition actually existed. It was not until I met with Dr Joe Albright that I began to receive a framework, a new name for the condition, and better understanding of what I was encountering in ministry.

Picture a ball that represents the soul. The mind, will, and emotions are all together in one sphere. Now imagine the ball's being divided exactly in half with a firm, wall-like membrane separating the halves. We will call one side the *dark side* and might even picture it black to indicate the difference. The other side is the *light side* or the core. In life the ball never rotates. The light side is always exposed and interacting directly with life events while the dark side is hidden and stays in the background. This side is called the "flipside" because it was created not as a result of trauma or abuse in one's own life experiences but rather because its source lies in the iniquity of previous generations and sin of the parent in rejecting the child.

The Scriptures state that the iniquity of the fathers can be passed down to the third or fourth generation (Exodus 20:5; Deuteronomy 5:9) The Hebrew word *avah* translated "iniquity" means *to bend, twist, or distort.* The literal meaning of the word *avah* means to turn upside down. This describes perfectly the condition of the personality created as a result of the iniquity of one's forefathers— upside down from their Christian core. Hence, the name flipside is an excellent descriptive term for the condition.

How is a flipside created? Although God is the One who knits us together in the womb, He is not the only one working. Immediately after conception, the ancestral spirit begins setting up his territory. He takes as his right the ancestral sin and is able to indwell the adamic nature (carnal nature) of the newly-conceived child. David

158

acknowledged that he was conceived in iniquity. While he was yet in his mother's womb, David was subject to demonic incursion.

When a person sins, he may allow a demonic spirit into his life. If he never puts that sin under the cross by confession, the demonic spirit remains in the family and passes down the family line (Exodus 34:7). When a sin passes from one generation to the next through the presence of a spirit, we call it an "ancestral spirit." The ancestral spirit is assigned to a child at the moment of conception and then awaits the opportunity to divide the child by creating a circumstance that causes the child in the womb to be damaged. This might occur, for instance, when the parents react and adjust to the news of a coming child. Negative words, verbal abuse, and physical altercations, drug abuse, child out of wedlock can be a devastating event for the child. These words, actions, and emotions can become the causal event that permits an ancestral spirit to gain the legal right in the person's life.

When the ancestral demon begins his work, he enters either by the right of a curse or by an ancestral sin. He essentially divides the person right in half and views the side he occupies as his creation. The person has in effect a multiple personality disorder (MPD) in which one side never comes out. Although flipsides typically do not come forward this does not mean they are not active. The flipside often controls the person's life. It may be extremely strong or very weak, but in either case the person will feel as though he simply cannot get his life together. For instance, on the very brink of success the person will find himself sabotaging his life.

A person with a flipside can also have many other parts created through traumatic events. The flipside, however, provides the base for the ancestral spirit. Unless the flipside is discovered and dealt with a person's freedom will never be realized.

Split-Souled

James 1:8 speaks of a "double-minded man, unstable in all of his ways." The Greek word translated "double-minded" is "dipsuchos."[37] The meaning is "split-souled" or "two-souled" and means, in context, a person who cannot make up his or her mind. People with flipsides are double-minded to the extreme and exhibit these characteristics because of the fact that most flipsides are not in Christ.

Because the ancestral demon attempts to take the person's formal name (given by the parents on the birth certificate), it tries to give the dark side a name that takes away any meaningful identity or gives it an identity that is demeaning. Some such names include: "no one," "nobody," "unwanted," "worthless," "wrong," "unloved," "shame," "dirty," " failure," "no name," "just me," "stubborn," "rebellion," or "bitterness."

Finding a flipside is a bit more difficult than finding other trauma-induced dissociations. The key to finding a flipside is to identify it by age. It is the same age as the core. It has a demeaning or reproachful identity and takes credit for all of the person's failures and sins. It will also bear many personality traits of the ancestral spirit rather than of the core personality.

Before trying to find the flipside I bind any ancestral spirit associated with it and the entire network and gatekeepers. I have discovered that the core can carry a separate ancestral system from the flipside. The enemy is a clever legalist. So in our initial prayer with a person I suspect has a flipside we include a binding of both the demonic system associated with the core and the demonic system associated with the flipside.

To begin locating the flipside I direct the person to close his eyes and monitor what happens inside. I say something such as:

> "I want to speak to the flipside of Bill. You are the same age as Bill and you have always been there. You control most of his life but seldom or never come forward. You are the one that has sabotaged Bill's life. Every time he gets his life together you do something to steal his success. You make him feel like a failure. You probably have a name like _____ (I go through the flipside list above)."

I am careful not to say this in a critical manner but instead share it with a matter-of-fact tone that leans toward compassion.

At this point, I typically ask the person if any of these names connect internally. Often one of the names will strike a nerve. On a few occasions the person has just popped out with the flipside name. If nothing comes up I say:

> "But that is not who you are. That is the enemy. You are actually no different from "Bill." In fact you have been deceived by the ancestral spirit, thinking his

thoughts and feeling his emotions. God was the One who knit you in the womb and He has a plan for you. He loves you and will perfect you. Every negative thing that you have ever done to "Bill," Jesus wants to take it to the cross, just as He does for Bill. You are truly a child of God, already seated in heavenly places, and a prince."

I continue by quoting Scriptures that declare his new identity in Christ and his future victory.

By this time the flipside will have surfaced in most cases. I then lead the flipside through a list of confessions in the core's life. Then I address the issue of forgiveness and make sure that the person has forgiven the critical offenders in his or her life. Once this has been done, I ask both sides if they are willing to fuse and integrate. I then pray for God to complete the work in a prayer similar to the one for sub-parts, such as: "Lord, I ask that you would take this flipside and allow it to fuse with the core where he or she belongs. Tear down the walls and barriers and allow it to become one with the core. I pray that You, Lord, will make this man or woman into the person You envisioned from the very beginning of time."

I once prayed with a woman who did not want the evil flipside to integrate with her core. I had to explain that the flipside was just like the core and not evil. The ancestral spirit was the one who all along had orchestrated the sabotage. It was also the culprit behind her exaggerated and distorted emotions and behavior.

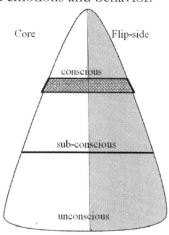

Figure 7: Flipside

Breaking Ancestral Rights

Then I have the person pray an ancestral confession from the Steps to Victory. (www.moriahfreedomministry.com)

"Father in heaven, I confess any and all sins of my ancestors and renounce all of those sins, known and unknown. (Neh 1:6, 7) I confess and renounce all forms of immorality, impurity, sensuality, idolatry, sorcery, enmities, strife, jealousy, outbursts of anger, disputes, dissentions, divorce, factions, lying, envying, and substance abuse. I confess and renounce any worship of any false gods. (Gal 5:19-21) I specifically renounce Baal, Ashterah, Mammon, Molech, Antichrist, and any other unholy pagan god. I confess any idol worship, dishonoring or rebelling against parents, stealing, injustice or violence against my brothers, incest, beastiality, false witness or denial of any other of God's ordinances and laws. I remove any curses and loose any binds that Satan or his demons may have directed against my family or my ministry. (Deut 27:15-26) I announce to Satan and all of his forces that Christ received every curse directed at me when he died on the cross. (Gal 3:13)

"I declare my family to be eternally and completely signed over and committed to the Lord Jesus Christ. By the authority that I have in Jesus Christ, I now command every enemy of the Lord Jesus Christ that is in or around me to leave my presence forever. I commit myself to my Heavenly Father to do His will from this day forward. In the name of Jesus I pray. I choose the fruit of the Spirit to reign in my soul and body. I choose to love others sacrificially, be joyful even in tribulation, and live in peace. I choose to be patient and show kindness toward others. I choose goodness and faithfulness, gentleness and self-control in my relationships with others, in the name of Jesus Christ I pray, amen. (Gal 5:22-23)"

After the person completes this prayer, the ancestral spirit will surface upon command. I then remove any remaining legal rights or strongholds.

Core Death

Whenever I pray for someone who has experienced Satanic Ritual Abuse (SRA), I always look for a part that has been "put to death." SRA survivors commonly testify about having experienced a ritual in which they were buried alive. They describe a ceremony in which as a young child they were placed in a box or coffin. Words and chants were spoken and, in some cases, drugs were administered. They were then lowered into a grave and could hear the dirt being shoveled onto the coffin.

The result of this ritual is that the core was put to sleep and a "false core" was resurrected. This false core is very weak in comparison to a real core. As the person grows up the real core cannot accept the Gospel because it thinks it is dead. While this does not prevent the person from accepting Christ in a sub-personality, it seems to weaken the overall will of the survivor. It also seems to surrender more ground to the enemy who thereby gains more strength in the victim's life.

Occasionally I see this same condition absent a testimony of ritual abuse. In these cases typically the person experienced a very significant rejection. For instance, Helen was only two years old when a part was created. Without a specific "buried alive" ritual as in SRA, Helen's damage occurred when she felt abandoned and rejected. She remembered or imagined being alone and crying and sobbing for many hours. She felt as though she had died. Later, as we prayed with her an enemy that entered at the same time was revealed whose identity and assignment was "devastation."

As a young adult Helen was introduced to the Gospel and accepted Jesus as her Savior in her false core. But she was never able to experience victory in her Christian walk. No matter what she did it always seemed to end in devastation. The enemy would never let her remember her successes, only her failures. As we prayed with her we found a little girl sub-personality whose assignment in life was to make sure that Helen's actions ended in devastation. The core thought she had "died" at two years old and a false core was created to carry out her life. The real core who was two years old, however, reigned emotionally in Helen driving her depression and feelings of devastation.

As I prayed with Helen we were able to bind up the enemy of devastation. While Helen could sense the part, it was not speaking. I had to lead her to break the lie of her being put to death and all covenants of death, including vows and oaths of silence. Then I had Helen ask the Lord to resurrect her, explaining that He could do it because He is the Lord of the resurrection. Once she did this the two-year-old core could speak. She was so depressed by the devastation that life had wrought on her that she began sobbing uncontrollably for 10–15 minutes.

The level of debilitation that a person with a "dead" core experiences is nearly identical to a "flipside." It literally devastates a victim.

Interjects

Many deliverance ministers have encountered an interesting phenomenon when praying with people who have come out of abusive occult activity, especially satanic ritual. They discover sub-personalities that have been created at some point in the person's life but not as a result of any traumatic event. That is, they were created without a precipitating traumatic experience. I have heard such parts referred to as "interjects" and have adopted that label. Unlike the flipside discussed in the previous chapter, interjects came into existence at a specific time (post-birth) in the person's life. The person will have no memory of any event that occurred to create them. They will also have no issues of unforgiveness or a stronghold. In other words, unlike other manifestations of the enemy (in trauma-induced parts or flipsides) interjects have no legal right to be or to stay in the person's life.

Why then do they exist? If a person has been abused, the demonic plan is to repeat that abuse over and over. Demonic spirits do not want a person ever to forget the abuse but rather to relive it through a demonic memory that mimics both the content and the emotion associated with the trauma. Since the enemy can affect emotions, his scheme is to cause the person to feel everything all over again—even down to the physical pain. In such cases the culprit is typically an enemy within the created pain parts. The part itself is not in pain; rather, the enemy is projecting the feelings of pain.

An interject is created in the image of the abuser. I prayed with a young lady named Elaine who had many parts. She referred to her voices as the "committee." As we prayed with her we found that she had a lot of unforgiveness. In leading her through the process we started in the core, directing her to forgive her mother and her father. As we spoke these words she heard a part say, "No you can't." We thought at first that it was a demon speaking and therefore issued the appropriate commands, but it was still there. As we addressed the part we found that it appeared to take on the identity of her mother. Elaine was very intimidated by her mother. I do not suspect that Elaine's mother was excessively abusive, but Elaine was very sensitive. In any event, internally a part was created that simulated her mother. No matter where Elaine went her mother was there to abuse her internally. What makes this especially insidious is that her mother may actually be a sweet, soft-spoken person trying her best as a parent not to hurt her daughter.

Many years ago I was praying with a young lady named Terry who was escaping from Satanic Ritual Abuse (SRA). Through the traumas she experienced during the SRA, demonic spirits had created interjects. As we prayed with Terry she would tell me to stop screaming. My prayer partner would look at her and me totally befuddled because I was speaking very softly. In counseling I always drop my voice because I am usually talking to parts that have been traumatized by loud voices and verbal abuse. As we continued to work with Terry, we discovered that internally a part representing me had been created. Every time she closed her eyes she would see an interject posing as me screaming and yelling at her. This was the first time I had encountered an interject that was created in adult life. I was never quite sure whether it was strictly a demonic creation or part of an cultic ritual. Terry was still involved in occult behavior even as she was trying to escape. She was being summoned demonically into cultic ritual because some of her parts were still in satanic agreement.

What do we do with interjects? I picture them as "puppet" characters with no inner content. Demons use them as a costume to hide their true identity. Fortunately, interjects are easily removed. Because there is no trauma or forgiveness to deal with in removing it is just a process of commanding. I bind and remove any demonic spirits who occupy the interjects. I have found that, unlike sub-personalities, no interjects seem to be able to accept Christ. This implies that since they were created demonically no measure of faith has been distributed to these parts, so I ask the Lord to remove the interject and send it to the pit. In Discussion with Charles Kraft, his approach has been to just dissolve them. Both techniques seem to work.

Chapter 3: Importance of Forgiveness

For most Christians this is probably the most important step. Unforgiveness is the cause of the enemy's foothold in Ephesians chapter 4: "Do not let the sun go down on your anger lest the enemy get a foothold."

Forgiveness is the subject of Jesus' parable after Peter asked Him how many times he had to forgive his brother—"up to seven times?" Jesus replied "seventy times seven" and then shared a parable about a master (the Lord) who wants to settle accounts with a slave (that's you and me).

> "Jesus *said to him, 'I do not say to you, up to seven times, but up to seventy times seven. For this reason the kingdom of heaven may be compared to a king who wished to settle accounts with his slaves. When he had begun to settle them, one who owed him ten thousand talents was brought to him. But since he did not have the means to repay, his lord commanded him to be sold, along with his wife and children and all that he had, and repayment to be made. So the slave fell to the ground and prostrated himself before him, saying, "Have patience with me and I will repay you everything." And the lord of that slave felt compassion and released him and forgave him the debt. But that

slave went out and found one of his fellow slaves who owed him a hundred denarii; and he seized him and began to choke him, saying, "Pay back what you owe." So his fellow slave fell to the ground and began to plead with him, saying, "Have patience with me and I will repay you." But he was unwilling and went and threw him in prison until he should pay back what was owed. So when his fellow slaves saw what had happened, they were deeply grieved and came and reported to their lord all that had happened. Then summoning him, his lord *said to him, "You wicked slave, I forgave you all that debt because you pleaded with me. Should you not also have had mercy on your fellow slave, in the same way that I had mercy on you?" And his lord, moved with anger, handed him over to the torturers until he should repay all that was owed him. My heavenly Father will also do the same to you, if each of you does not forgive his brother from your heart.'" (Matthew 18:22-35)

Notice how the first slave entreated the master and He forgave him his debt. The master represents our Father in heaven (whom we owe an infinite debt). We see this connection in the last verse. Another slave, however, owed the first slave a small amount, analogous to someone we may hold in unforgiveness (i.e., compared to what we owe God and what He has to forgive us for, what others owe us and what we have to forgive them for is minuscule!). The second slave entreated the first slave to forgive him, but the first slave refused and sent him to jail. This debt is analogous to our unforgiveness and is pictured as a debt. Someone who has unforgiveness is essentially saying the other person owes him and must pay him back. When the master found out about the unforgiveness of the first slave he became angry and sent tormenters, jailers, or torturers (depending on the translation). In Ephesians 4 we see that these are demonic spirits sent to torment the first slave until the debt is forgiven. As the parable concludes Jesus says, "in the same way the Father will do to you if you do not forgive your brother from your heart."

The Greek word for prison used in this parable is translated as "under watch" or "under guard" in other Scriptures. The idea is that if we do not forgive our trespassers, we are in bondage guarding that prisoner (i.e., the jailer is in prison, too). Everywhere we go in life we are shackled together with the persons we refuse to forgive and we drag them through our life. In some cases the trespasser is long ago-deceased and yet we continue to remain in bondage due to our unforgiveness. Some events will act as triggers and cause us to look back at that person who has hurt us. But until we choose to forgive, that person will remain forever connected to us.

Again, like the Ephesians passage, we see the importance of forgiveness and the discipline we will face if we do not forgive. The second point I want you to see is that we, as slaves, are in bondage. When unforgiveness occurs in a relationship both individuals are affected. Thus when we forgive one another freedom comes to families and friends!

In the Old Testament Saul held anger against David. From that day forward, an evil spirit tormented Saul. It would come upon him without warning and he would experience terror or rage. We see the account in 1 Samuel 18:

> "The women sang as they played, and said, 'Saul has slain his thousands, And David his ten thousands.' Then Saul became very angry, for this saying displeased him; and he said, 'They have ascribed to David ten thousands, but to me they have ascribed thousands. Now what more can he have but the kingdom?' Saul looked at David with suspicion from that day on. Now it came about on the next day that an evil spirit from God came mightily upon Saul, and he raved in the midst of the house, while David was playing the harp with his hand, as usual; and a spear was in Saul's hand. Saul hurled the spear for he thought, 'I will pin David to the wall.' But David escaped from his presence twice." (1 Samuel 18:7-11)

Forgiveness begins with the will. ***It is not a feeling!*** Jesus commands us to forgive, and He will discipline us if we do not forgive. Jesus makes a very strong statement about unforgiveness right after the Lord's Prayer. In the prayer He has already told us to forgive, but then He further emphases the point.

> "For if you forgive men for their transgressions, your heavenly Father will also forgive you. But if you do not

forgive men, then your Father will not forgive your transgressions." (Matthew 6:14-15)

Although unforgiveness is not a matter that will separate us from our salvation, it will certainly hinder our full relationship with Christ. Strongholds of unforgiveness can establish deep roots of bitterness that will torment our souls. The enemies attracted to footholds of unforgiveness claim to bring all sorts of physical infirmities. In the Scriptures we are taught that bitterness brings defilement.

> "See to it that no one comes short of the grace of God;
> that no root of bitterness springing up causes trouble,
> and by it many be defiled." (Hebrews 12:15)

Some of you may ask why unforgiveness is so important that the Lord makes an extreme point and invokes such severe discipline. The answer that seems to satisfy most people is this: The Lord came to die for our sins on the cross. When we do not forgive we are working for the wrong kingdom. We, like Jesus, are to pick up our cross and forgive others. The phrase "pick up your cross daily" in this context does not mean simply to "do what Christ wants me to do," as is usually taught. "Picking up my cross" means to forgive others daily, just as Jesus forgave me.

Forgiveness is not:
Forgiveness is not tolerance
Forgiveness is not trust
Forgiveness is not a feeling
Forgiveness is not forgetting
Forgiveness is not generosity
Forgiveness is not enabling

Forgiveness is:
Forgiveness is a decision
Forgiveness is an act of the will
Forgiveness is a full pardon
Forgiveness is obedience
Forgiveness is picking up our cross
Forgiveness is freedom.

"And so, as those who have been chosen of God, holy and beloved, put on a heart of compassion, kindness, humility, gentleness and patience; bearing with one another, and forgiving each other, whoever has a complaint against anyone; just as the Lord forgave you, so also should you...." (Colossians 3:12-13)

I often encounter two lies that cause opposition to forgiving. The first lie involves trust. We are led to believe that if we forgive then that gives the person the freedom to abuse us again. The enemy very craftily ties trust and forgiveness together. The truth is that trust and forgiveness are not connected. Trust is earned; forgiveness is automatic. When David could no longer trust Saul not to try to kill him, David escaped to the wilderness. This is a good example for us to follow. When it is unsafe to trust, we should not take revenge but instead remove ourselves from the target area. David would then reenter Saul's presence at different times to test whether Saul had forgiven. In Saul's case, he was never able to release his unforgiveness.

The second lie we believe is that if we forgive then the other person gets away free and clear without any consequences. Part of this lie is that we believe that the person we do not forgive is somehow punished by our unforgiveness. The truth is that that we are the only one suffering from our unforgiveness. The other spiritual truth to understand is that as long as *we* are holding the person in "shackles" God leaves him alone. In other words while the person is in our "jail" God does not discipline him in relation to us. When we let him go we leave room for the Lord's discipline (Romans 12:19).

In addition to forgiving others we need to ask forgiveness of those we have offended. Before we even come to worship the Lord we need both to forgive and to reconcile with our brothers.

"If therefore you are presenting your offering at the altar, and there remember that your brother has something against you, leave your offering there before the altar, and go your way; first be reconciled to your brother, and then come and present your offering." (Matthew 5:23-24)

When we initiate through reconciliation and seek forgiveness from the other person we are releasing them from bondage.

The question for many of us is not a matter of *whether* we are to forgive but rather *how* we can forgive. I have found it very helpful to begin the process by stating out loud, "I choose to forgive _____ in the name of Jesus."

By approaching forgiveness with a statement of intent (that is, *I choose*), it seems to back the enemy off of the foothold he has gained. If the person is unable or unwilling to say the words (as is often the case) then I bind the enemy of rage or anger in Jesus' name. They will then easily be able to say the words. Note that at this point it is only a declaration and not from the heart. It is not necessary for the other person to know that we are forgiving him or her. In other words, our unforgiveness is not in any way conditional on the other person. In fact, the person we are forgiving may be unaware that he has offended. He may have passed away or for some other reason no longer be available. This does not change our need to forgive.

I ask the person to repeat the words of forgiveness until his feelings line up with the intent of his will. This is usually followed by tears and a physical feeling of a burden being lifted. We continue this process until the person feels entirely free. I have seen some individuals repeat this statement of intent 20-30 times before the hold is broken. When finally the person is free the emotion associated with the memory is gone. The person is now able to think about the person and the events and though the memory is intact the feelings of anger, rage, frustration, and bitterness are gone. It should be like the memory of any other event the person experienced or witnessed.

Chapter 4: Tracy's Inner Healing Begins

Jim: It was the third time we met. I knew that a little girl had surfaced the previous times Tracy and I had met. She would cry and talk, but no real healing had yet been accomplished. I could tell that she did not yet trust me.

Tracy came to this third meeting armed with some critical help from a source I never expected. She had received an email from one of her former ministers who had been given a "word of knowledge." Over the years I have learned to test such "words" and discovered that in many instances they are the turning point. This was one of those times. Tim Williams gave her a name "Clarissa." So during the session I asked if a little girl by the name of Clarissa would be willing to speak to me, and out came the little part who was surprised that we knew her name.

Tracy: As Jim spoke to Clarissa I felt her surface and the emotions came. She was finally seen and acknowledged. Clarissa told Jim of her pain, how she felt about life, and her fear of men. Interestingly, as I reviewed my journals from 17 years ago, I could see that Clarissa had been writing.

"Clarissa" speaks (journal entry 1993): I am at my wits end to comprehend how I am to love a man. I ask myself why I want it anyway. I desire women's bodies, emotionality, care, and sensitivity. Why should I want men when I have that? The only conclusion for me is that I must know God's will for my life. I refuse to stop short again. My fear is that again I will make efforts to move towards what I believe to be God's best for a woman and all I will get back is trying without emotional change. I am afraid my conclusion for my life is that I have no choice but lesbianism. I have said to almost everyone I know that from now on I refuse to half-exist or live on a level pleasing to others but unhappy to me. I refuse to marry if I am not in love, I cannot live a lie unto myself. To "just do it" means giving away your soul. My desire is that God works with me, through my pain, misunderstanding and that my life choices become choices that are natural to me. I am so afraid I will never love again the way I loved Char. I keep thinking life could not be so cruel as to keep me from love but now I do not put it past God or life.

Tracy: It was not until this day when I was working with Jim that I understood why I, a grown woman, felt young in so many circumstances. The sub-part, Clarissa, was in constant flux and surfacing based on the trigger, and this was coupled with the enemy's work of heightening my emotions way beyond normal affect. It seemed as though the Lord had an agenda regarding how He wanted my parts to surface, with Clarissa[38] being the largest and most dominant sub-part that drove me toward homosexuality. I could feel Clarissa rise up inside, full of tears, wanting to be noticed and loved. She was hurt, afraid, ashamed, and yet, when Jim would speak to Clarissa, she would present herself with tears, hungry for attention.

Jim: Finding Clarissa was the first step in the process. As I worked with her I wanted to lead her to Christ as soon as possible. For some reason, though, she was not easily won over, so I spent many hours on inner healing, especially related to her forgiveness of her parents. Later I learned that she had a protector that was preventing her from accepting Christ and would sometimes interfere with the healing process.

Clarissa also helped me to link to other sub-personalities. Often a part will be able to "see" inside and will aid in the location of other sub-parts. Leading Clarissa to Christ was a major step in Tracy's progress. Clarissa did not trust Christ since she felt that "He would draw her in to then destroy her."

Tracy let me read her journals, and I was amazed at her spiritual maturity and struggles with the dilemma of "being gay" and being right with God. Page after page over many years she had recorded her daily pleas for God's help, searching for the meaning of her brokenness and struggles with her dysfunctional gay relationships that never satisfied the emptiness she felt. Embedded in these journal entries were Scriptures of encouragement and guidance that helped her find a path to her ultimate freedom. As I read through her journals I could see other parts writing.

> **"Outcast" speaks** (journal entry 1993): I am angry at God, for letting me be this way, for allowing me to feel so empty, so alone. I have nobody. I cannot relate to anyone, I do not fit. The Christian mold is not for me. I feel I need to conform to a way of thinking and acting that is not me. There is a Christian subculture that I adhered to in college: dress a certain way, act and think a certain way. I hate it! I just want to be me and a Christian. I may dress different, be different, listen to different music but feel whole inside and relate to others as me.

Tracy: When I was in high school I went through a punk rocker phase. When I was in the gay lifestyle I adopted a harder persona to cover my hurts. I tried to not care that other people would look at me and comment about my being a "dyke." The sub-part felt out of sync with straight people, and so I made sure I was an outcast. This not only had to do with the enemy's attack on my appearance, but I was also told that I was not like others or that I did not fit.

Jim: Outcast needed to hear that Jesus did not think of her as an outcast. He loved her just as she was. God wanted her to be unique and gift her in a special way, but he also wanted her included in the body of Christ. It was important for Outcast to know that she was not different from others and that God did not like labels that made her different. She was a child of God, a princess waiting to be seated in

175

heavenly places. Outcast was the "pearl of great price," the "treasure hid in the field." Most important, Outcast was already accepted in the heavenly family. There was nothing more that she needed to do to be accepted.

> **"T2" speaks** (journal entry 1991): Talked with mom today and asked her if she would just listen to me. I told her that she has no right or place to judge me as I do not have the right to judge or blame her. My life is my own and she cannot live vicariously through me or anyone. Mom said, "I just see you messing your life up and sometimes it takes someone to pick themselves up by the seat of their pants and move on."

Tracy: T2 was the protector and the one that drove me to do the things I accomplished. I likely became an attorney because T2 was determined to succeed at something. She was not going to be a failure, which is what she heard growing up. Neither her emotions nor others' judgment would stop T2. She was not only a sort of alter ego to the sensitive "Tracy" but felt like "T" meant "Terminator."

T2 was cold and calculated and did not feel emotion, even if it was required. She protected the system from overload and was the sub-part that solved the family's problems when needed. I remember when Jim called T2 forward and discovered that Clarissa was hiding behind T2. Although Clarissa would surface fully in me, T2 stayed in the background and controlled events. In my mind I could see the sub-part with Clarissa hiding behind her. As the protector, T2 would not integrate into the core until she knew that Clarissa went with her and that she would be safe.

Jim: T2's independent nature made her emotionally strong, and Jesus was not necessary to her way of operating and thinking. My main focus of ministry to T2 was to show her that although she was very capable in the physical realm her inability to be armored up made her ineffective in protecting Tracy or Clarissa in the spiritual realm. Once T2 was convinced that Jesus could help her in being a better protector, it was just a matter of time before she accepted Him as her Savior. After the Holy Spirit enters into a part, truth is accepted readily and healing follows swiftly.

Tracy also had a flipside that operated to keep her alone, isolated, and feeling like and outcast.

Tracy: The flipside named Alone was black and white. I was able to see a split directly down the middle of my body, one side being normal and one side being totally dark and seemingly isolated and numbed. The flipside operated to keep me alone. This enemy controlled all the other spirits and parts that operated to keep me isolated.

> **Alone speaks**: For my entire life I have been alone, isolated and anonymous. I will grow old with no one knowing me or wanting to know me, to love me or to grow old with me. At my age it is too late. My emotions are so painful that I want to disappear and give up. Why fight this fight any further since all that happens is that I grow older with no one who wants me. I am so tired of doing this life alone.

Jim: Finding the flipside was fairly easy with Tracy once we suspected that she existed. I began addressing the part as I usually do flipsides— telling her that she controls the core's life and has sabotaged every major success in Tracy's life. I said it in a matter-of-fact way, not with an accusing tone. I then switched to the influence of the ancestral spirit and told the flipside that it had been operating in the emotions and thoughts of the head demonic spirit. I described her as a part of the core and not different from Tracy.

After preparing the flipside with this background, I went for the part by addressing it by name, suggesting typical identities. I asked her if her name was "no one," "no body," "shame," "rebellion," "unloved," "unwanted".... After a few moments Tracy opened her eyes and said "Alone." Alone was the key to most of Tracy's feelings. It was the way she felt in relation to her dad and her mom. She was isolated, abandoned, and alone. These three words summarized her failed relationships with every partner and even all of her friends. Although she had maintained many childhood friends she still perceived herself as alone. This was also the description of her relationship with God. She felt that God had abandoned her, left her isolated and alone. No one would rescue her.

Tracy: Although we have integrated more than 40 sub-parts, approximately 13 major personalities had distinct names and took on the functional identity. As a result, some of the parts were named Anonymous, Devastation, Despair, Check Out, Worthless, Hopeless, Nothing, and Sad.

One of my sub-parts was named Trace and had a male identity. Trace did not want to feel vulnerable and operated like a boy or tomboy to keep Tracy safe from hurtful circumstances. She was 16 years old and would have preferred to have male parts. Trace was a coping part and justified the right to be in a relationship with a woman because somehow Trace knew that a man should have been a part of the relationship.

Jim: Often we will encounter parts that will carry opposite-sex identities. Rarely are they the cause of gay behavior. They are typically formed because the person feels deficient in some way. Either the person's sexuality was not affirmed as a child or the person may have felt that it would be better to be the opposite sex for some internal function. Women will often have a male part as a protector because it makes more sense in our culture – "men protect." I have heard another client say that "sometimes it is safer to be a man." Although there were many other parts in Tracy, all followed the same patterns for healing.

Part IV: Casting out Demons

James L. Hanley & C. Tracy Kayser

Chapter 1: Dealing with Demons

While the enemy has essentially been defeated when the inner healing is complete, I usually take the person through a spiritual inventory such as the *Steps to Victory*.[39] I want to make sure that the whole person has confessed and had an opportunity to give their sins to God. The *Steps to Victory* is an extremely effective tool to achieve that goal. Once the person has gone through the *Steps*, I still address the enemy for two reasons. First, there may be some sin issue that has been overlooked. Second, I want to expose the strongholds and help the person to overcome his or her unbiblical thought patterns.[40]

Step 1: Addressing the Spirit

Early on in the ministry my approach was to find the most powerful demon and call him forth using the method Dr. Charles Kraft teaches, which is to address each demon in succession. My standard procedure now is to address all of the demons collectively under the head demon of highest authority, but on occasion I will address the demons individually. Dr. Charles Kraft's book *Defeating Dark Angels* is the most helpful resource on the topic of addressing demons.

Sometimes the person will go into the background, and the enemy will come forward. At other times the enemy will just speak to the person's mind. Either way is acceptable. Then I begin my interrogation with the objective of finding the "legal right"—that is, discovering how the enemy got in. Usually the enemy gained entrance through a sin the person committed. If the person was abused or traumatized, the sin is not the event itself (for which the person was not responsible) but more likely the sin of unforgiveness.

The first thing I always do is to bind the enemy to the truth. Demons will often try to distract us by engaging in conversation—as a diversionary tactic to keep us off-topic. I do not want to find out any information that demons have on other subjects. I am just commanding to find the information I want to know in order to secure the person's freedom. Since demons are liars, just like a police interrogation with a guilty or unreliable subject in the temporal realm, I expect false information or, at best, distortions. We have some tools, however, to ply the enemy into speaking the truth.

Step 2: Distinguishing between Sub-parts and Demons

I begin the process of determining whether I am dealing with a sub-personality or a demon. Sometimes at this point I may not get the enemy at all. If I get a deceptive response or the voice does not bind to truth it may be a sub-personality.

Occasionally a sub-part will think it is a demon. They are often created in demonic confusion and can "fellowship" with demons. Sub-parts may think that they themselves are a demon or want you to think they are a demon. A critical distinction is that sub-personalities will be able to say the phrase "Jesus came in the flesh" whereas demons cannot make this claim. What's more, sub-parts will have no memory of heaven whereas demons will have a clear memory of the last time they were in heaven.

If the voice is a sub-part rather than a demon I return to the healing path described previously.

If it is a demon that is just trying to delay or deceive, I continue with the use of threats to get the demons to comply with my commands.

Because there is limited scriptural authority and I strive always to be doctrinally sound, I couch my threats in conditional statements. The demoniac of the Gerasenes called Legion was fearful of two things that Jesus might do: (1) cast them out of the area or (2) throw them into the pit before it was their time. In Jude and 2 Peter we see that some demonic angels received that latter penalty when "in the same way as Sodom and Gomorrah" they went after strange flesh. This may be the result of the odd story recounted in Genesis 6:1-6.

The demons seem to think the events are connected, but we do not want to create a doctrine of demons here so I will leave it to theologians to debate the passages. What I do know is this: When I tell a demon that if he does not cooperate I will ask Jesus to throw him into the pit before his time, the demon does not like it and will usually cough up the truth. Is the threat valid? I am not sure, but Jesus *is* sure so I let Him decide and the demons respond.

Once I issue a command that binds the enemy to the truth and the demon disobeys or lies, he may have broken a covenant with God and is truly in jeopardy. In the spiritual realm demons must follow certain rules or consequences such as those Jude and Peter related are invoked. In the book of Job we see that Satan and demons must report to God. In relation to Job, Satan could only do what God allowed. Many times in Scripture we see demons coming directly from the throne of God (1 Samuel 18:7-10).

Step 3: Legal Rights

The way the enemy gets into a person's life is through a legal right, which is an unconfessed sin. I have two options: (1) I can either have the demon reveal the sin or (2) I can take the person through the *Steps to Victory* (moriahfreedomministry.com) to collectively remove all demonic rights.

Even if a person has already gone through the *Steps to Victory* (moriahfreedomministry.com) before inner healing and integration, I recommend repeating the process now that the core has incorporated many sub-personalities that may have been involved in various sins. This is especially true of coping personalities.

Step 4: Strongholds

When we finally get the demon to declare the sin issues, if any, and the person confesses all that the enemy claims are his rights, then I command the enemy to tell me its lies. These are the strongholds that the enemy has led the person to believe in lieu of the truth from God's word. A typical stronghold might be: "I'm guilty, ashamed, or defiled."

In order to nullify these strongholds we merely quote God's Word. It trumps the enemy's lies. It is important to note that the enemy will share many things that are true in the temporal realm. A person may really be alone…. But God will never leave her. A person may have an unacceptable body…. But God will give him a new one.

If I sense that the person is struggling with a particular issue I will call forward the spirit involved in that behavior and take it through the litany of lies, which will usually be only four or five in number. When I call it forward I make certain to bring forward all spirits involved.

For example, many rage or anger enemies may be involved in a person's tirades, especially if there are many people to forgive. I have found that this step is very helpful in getting the person's awareness of what he is thinking versus what the enemy is doing to his emotions and thought life.

In praying with my co-author Tracy, I felt it was very important that she hear from the enemy's mouth that he was the source of the unwanted sexual attraction to women in both her thoughts and her emotions. It was a revelation for Tracy to understand and later experience that her emotions could align with her biblical understanding, which was heterosexual attraction.

Many in the gay community have been taught that they were "born that way" or that homosexuality is genetic. Given the work of flipsides and ancestral spirits, this may be a true statement relative to their birth but not true at the point of conception. Remember that ancestral spirits can only begin work on a developing child after conception. A sexual ancestral spirit may begin to establish a flipside just after conception that perverts a person's sexual orientation. While same-sex attraction may be all the person has ever experienced, the spiritual truth is that God never intended him or her to be that way.

When I began to pray with Tracy I was very quick to point out that I did not want to force her to behave in a different way. My objective was to get her emotions to line up with God's word. That was going to be the goal of deliverance.

Stronghold lies are essentially our unbelief of certain Christian truths. These lies are so ingrained that we cannot distinguish them from truth. The lie has become our "truth." We then operate in life as though the lie was the truth and it is almost impossible to accept God's truth.

"….Indeed, did not all those who came out of Egypt led by Moses? And with whom was He angry for forty years? Was it not with those who sinned, whose bodies fell in the wilderness? And to whom did He swear that they would not enter His rest, but to those who were disobedient? So we see that they were not able to enter because of **unbelief**." (Hebrews 3:16-19) (emphasis added)

Notice that God indicts Israel for both their disobedience and their unbelief. Unbelief is the area where a stronghold reigns. As we continue to look at Hebrews we see that the Christian walk is a process of grabbing onto the promises of God in order to enter into His rest. It is necessary to expel the enemy with the truth to gain maturity in Christ as we rest in His promise.

> "Therefore, let us fear if, while a promise remains of entering His rest, any one of you may seem to have come short of it. For indeed we have had good news preached to us, just as they also; but the word they heard did not profit them, because it was not united by faith in those who heard." (Hebrews 3:1-2)

The first promise we grab onto in the process of entering into rest is the promise of the Gospel. We find that in every area of spiritual struggle we must overcome by grabbing onto a promise of God. Secular life is filled with lies that must be overcome to gain Christian maturity.

> "For in it the righteousness of God is revealed from faith to faith…." (Romans 1:17)

We come to Christ by faith, and we grow in maturity by extending our faith. Each promise that we obtain is breaking a stronghold of the enemy.

The enemy primarily attacks our thought and emotional life in this area. If the enemy is causing us fear then we might quote the Scripture "God did not give me a spirit of fear but of power, love and a sound mind" (1 Timothy 1:7). Another lie of the enemy is "that God's word will return void." The truth is that His word will not return void but in fact will shatter these strongholds. Once the legal rights are removed and no inner parts remain this process is the only remaining step.

Notice two things about pulling down strongholds. First, we are taking the word of God and personifying it by declaring it in the first person (e.g., "God did not give *me* a spirit of fear but He gave me power, love, and a sound mind"). Second, we need to declare it until we believe it. It is not something we just naturally do with one attempt. We have repeated the lies over and over for years. Now we have to focus on the truth, repeat it, study it, think about it, and inhale it until we are transformed (Romans 12:1-2).

Simple confession of sin is all it takes to remove a legal right. It takes determination, on the other hand, to defeat a stronghold. The enemy's legal right will be nullified at the first declaration of confession and the truth, just as Satan was silenced in the wilderness as Jesus quoted Scriptures in context. Our fleshly nature, on the other hand, requires persistence and determination to break through to freedom.

Step 5: His Final Gasp

A sign that the enemy is ready to leave is when he has nothing more to say but lies of the following type: "She's mine"; "He doesn't want me to leave"; "She loves me"; "He can't cope without me." The enemy will try these desperate ploys in his final gasp. At this point I have the person merely reject the enemy. The prayer might be something such as this: "Jesus bought me with His shed blood on the cross. I am not yours. I belong to Jesus. I do not want you or your false protection. I want you out of my life in Jesus' name."

Once the legal rights and strongholds are broken and the enemy is no longer claiming any ground, I have the enemy remove any curses it placed on the person or the family. I make it declare that it will go to the foot of Jesus and never come back. At that point, if the enemy has taken over, I ask the person to come forward and make the command himself to rebuke the enemy and command the demonic spirit to go away. I have the person being delivered do this last part because it seems to be more powerful.

I continue to address the enemies until all have been dealt with. In most cases 5-15 major demons will need to be cast out. I believe that although more might be in the system God usually wraps them up with the main suspects. I forbid them or any like them to return.

For the past 18 years I have used this process with only a few minor changes. I no longer command the enemy one by one but instead use the *Steps to Victory* (moriahfreedomministry.com) and have found that I can address one head demon. This head demon is typically the one carrying the formal name on the person's birth certificate, and

I can find all the information necessary from that one spirit. The head demon knows all the lies and strongholds or can find the information. I will silence all enemies except the head demon.

At this point in the process I am not having a conversation with the spirit but rather commanding it. I find out any final legal rights or strongholds. When the enemy runs out of claims his last statement is something such as "I'll never leave," or "he needs me." At that point I have the person command the enemy to leave and issue a denial of the enemy's last claim. The person will seem to know when the enemy is gone.

Step 6: Removing Curses and Demonic Ailments

In the final stage of casting out the enemy, I address the demon and have it say, "I remove all curses that I or my demonic forces have placed on _____ [the person's name] and his or her family in Jesus' name."

Then I have the enemy list any physical illness or conditions that he causes, takes credit for, or enhances. I cancel all the enemy's assignments. If a demon is claiming that he brought an illness into the person's life, I have him declare what percentage of the affliction he has caused. If he claims it all (100%) the person is typically fully healed from that illness.

At this point we are finished *unless* the client has children under the age of accountability. In Exodus no children under the age of 20 were held accountable for the sins and unbelief of the adult generation. They were all allowed to follow Joshua into the Promised Land. If we find there are children who meet this criteria then I add the prayer in the next section before we cast the enemy out.

If the person has no children or they are grown they will have to pursue their own deliverance. I then have the person command the enemy to leave and go to the foot of Jesus. I have them forbid him or any like him to return.

Praying for Children and Seniors

1 Corinthians 7:14 says that a believing spouse makes the child holy. Because of a parent's spiritual authority over a child, it is not necessary in most cases to pray with children directly. I have found that I can call up any spirit who is affecting children through the parent.

I call up the head demon of highest authority using the formal name of the child on his or her birth certificate and bind the network and gatekeepers. I then interrogate the enemy to determine any damage that has been done. I have the enemy revoke any curses: "I remove any curse that I or my demons have placed over this child in Jesus' name." I then ask the angels of God to sweep the house of the child clean and to fill the territory the enemy vacated with the Holy Spirit.

Most issues with children are related to fear and night terrors. Once a child takes spiritual authority the enemy is dealt a swift blow. God really honors the prayers of children so I have the parents teach them to rebuke "in Jesus' name."

Many years ago a young man named Don came to me concerned about his mother. She was in an assisted living home but was experiencing demonic attacks at night. What she was describing was a spiritual sexual contact. Don could not find anyone from his own church who knew what to do and was referred to me through a former client.

At the time I was not sure what I could do but I suggested we try. Don and I went to the home and I talked to his mother for a while. Her health was extremely deteriorated, and I could see that she would not be able to help us in making affirmations and prayers. I told Don that he might have spiritual authority because she was a family member under his authority. I asked Don to read through the *Steps to Victory* (moriahfreedomministry.com) on his mother's behalf and she came free. Later she had a physical recovery and was with us for many more years during which she never had another spiritual assault.

Testing Spiritual Gifting and Prophecies

One of the most important issues in working with persons from charismatic churches or backgrounds is to test spiritual gifts, tongues, prophecies, dreams, and visions. I have found that many of these manifestations are not from the Lord.

I believe in spiritual gifting and believe it is for our time. Sadly, however, many well-meaning Christians are operating in false gifting. These people are not evil, but they have been deceived.

When I first began my ministry I was praying for a woman named Margo who was hearing voices. A woman named Donna had befriended her and prayed with Margo for months. Somehow they found out about Moriah Ministry and called for an appointment.

As Donna and I prayed for Margo we were able to get the demons removed. At the conclusion of our ministry time, Donna began praying in tongues. Although I had heard about tongues I had never seen or heard anyone pray that way and assumed that Donna was just worshipping the Lord.

After a few minutes Margo grimaced and said "the demon is back." Surprised, I went after it to find out what legal right it was claiming. The spirit spoke and declared that it had been invited back. "How?" I asked, binding it to the truth and commanding in Jesus' name. It finally spit out that Donna had invited it back. At the time this was very confusing to me. I asked Donna not to pray and was able to cast the enemy out again. This time is stayed out.

I Immediately began to probe this anomaly. I was certain that Donna was a Christian, but I had not yet encountered a Christian with a demonic tongue. We concluded that Donna's tongue might not be from the Lord. As I commanded the spirit that spoke in a tongue to come forward Donna recognized that a spirit was there. It admitted being a demonic spirit—not the Holy Spirit. That day we renounced the spirit and commanded it out of her life.

The incident drove me to a thorough study of this confusing situation. The result was that I discovered one of the most formidable tools that we have in spiritual warfare. Neil Anderson had recorded an encounter with a false tongue in a young man whom he called Alvin. He recorded the event in *The Bondage Breaker*.

> "Recently a man in his thirties was referred to me. Alvin was discouraged and defeated. For several years he believed he had a special gift of prophecy from God. He was invited to church after church to speak as an oracle for God by prophesying in his unique way. But over a period of months his personal life began to fall apart. Alvin eventually reached the point where he could no longer function in society and he began to withdraw from people completely. By the time he came to see me he had been unemployed for two years, he was being cared for by his father, and he was a slave to prescription drugs.

> "Alvin and I read 1 Thessalonians 5:19-21: 'Do not put out the Spirit's fire; do not treat prophecies with

contempt .Test everything. Hold on to the good' (NIV).

"I said, 'Alvin, I'm not against prophecy; it's a spiritual gift. But Satan can counterfeit spiritual gifts and deceive us into believing they're from God. That's why the Scriptures instruct us to put everything to the test.

"After a lengthy discussion about false prophets and teachers, Alvin admitted, 'I think my problems began when I failed to test the "gifts" of tongues and prophecy conferred on me by false teachers. Not only was I deceived, but I have deceived others myself.'

"'Would you be willing to put your gift of tongues to the test?' I asked. I assured Alvin that I was interested in putting the spirit to the test, not him. Alvin really wanted to be free of deception and right with God. 'Yes,' he answered. I instructed Alvin to begin praying aloud in his 'spiritual language.' As he began to chant an unintelligible prayer, I said, 'In the name of Christ and in obedience to God's Word, I command you, spirit, to identify yourself.' Alvin stopped in the middle of his chanting and said, 'I am he.' At this point a novice may have been tempted to take off his shoes, thinking he was on holy ground. But I continued, 'Was born under Pilate, buried, raised on the third day, and who now sits at the right hand of the Father?' Alvin almost shouted the response: 'No! Not he!'

"…I am not against spiritual gifts, even prophesy and tongues. But I am committed to obeying Scripture, and 1 Corinthians 14:39 says, 'Desire earnestly to prophesy, and do not forbid to speak in tongues.' But Scripture also requires that all spiritual phenomena be tested." [41]

I use the same method to test any revelation that might be masquerading as Christ. In the example above, Anderson applies the test to two aspects of revelation—tongues and prophesy.

I also use the test in a more extended way. Charismatic Christians will sometimes share that there are two types of tongues.

One is a tongue that requires interpretation for corporate worship. The other tongue is the person's private prayer language. They claim that this second type of tongues will excuse them from the test of interpretation Paul prescribed in 1 Corinthians 14:26-28. Although personally I have a difficult time validating the second type of tongues scripturally, I can still use 1 John 4:1-4 to test either tongue. In either case the spirit behind the tongue should be the Holy Spirit and subject to testing. I also use it to test dreams and visions.

My approach, like Neil Anderson's, is to get the tongue operating. Once it begins I then ask permission to test it and for it to switch to my language. If it is the Lord, He will shift to English because He has commanded me to test Him (1 Thessalonians 5:18-20).

I will then challenge the tongue to say, "Jesus came in the flesh" (1 John 4:1-4). If it is the Lord I will immediately hear "Jesus came in the flesh." Usually a few more phrases will be added. (i.e., "I am the Alpha and the Omega," "born of a virgin," etc.). If it is not the Lord the communication may cease or the spirit will say something such as "Yes" or some other indirect response. I have often had the tongue curse at me, which surprises the person who is speaking. Sometimes the tongue will just continue without acknowledging the question. Any of these latter responses exposes the antichrist spirit. I have the person renounce it and remove any curses that it has spoken using the client's voice.

If I am testing a prophecy, dream, or vision, I call in the spirit that gave the revelation. Then, as in the case of tongues, I challenge the spirit to declare that "Jesus came in the flesh." Since the Holy Spirit is in each Christian, He will reveal himself in us and we will know in our spirit.

Let me share an example of how this might work. As a pastor, I often have people come to me with "a word from the Lord." Since the Lord has commanded us to test the Spirit, I say to the person: "Let's test it." I may ask for another person to join us. Then I say, "Spirit that brought that word: Does that spirit confess that Jesus came in the flesh?" At that point we are usually all in agreement with what we thought or heard in our spirit. God does not want us to be deceived. He will allow us to test Him this way. In fact, we literally quench the Spirit if we do not test Him (1 Thessalonians 5:18-20).

If the test fails I make sure that the person who brought it is not embarrassed or in any way demeaned. Rather, I use it as a teaching opportunity. My conviction is that the more we test, the more we will hear true words from the Lord.

A more troubling case I came across in my research was an account in *He Came to Set the Captives Free* by Rebecca Brown, M.D. Dr. Brown's co-author Elaine records eight ways that as a satanist she would infiltrate churches and try to destroy their ministries. The first step is recorded as follows:[42]

#1) Profession of Faith

First of all the satanist must make a "profession of faith." He or she must pretend to be saved in order to gain credibility with the church people. In churches who have altar calls, the person will go forward, usually with tears, and pretend to "get saved." If the particular church is a charismatic church which places great emphasis on the gift of speaking in tongues, the satanist will speak in tongues. This is no problem, demons can speak in tongues very easily. Remember that when I was indwelt by Mann-Chan I was able to address any of the foreign dignitaries in their own language fluently. This is why the Lord places such emphasis on interpretation:

"When ye come together ... If any man speak in an unknown tongue, let it be by two or at the most by three, and that by course; and let one interpret. But if there be no interpreter, let him keep silence in the church; and let him speak to himself, and to God." 1 Corinthians 14:26-28.

Alas, how much damage is done because churches do not heed this simple warning. It is the custom in charismatic churches for many people to speak and pray in tongues at the same time without interpretation during their services and prayer meetings. Satanists take great advantage of this. During the time I served Satan, I spoke in tongues regularly in all the meetings and prayer meetings, so did the other satanists I was working with. No one interpreted. We were cursing the church, the pastor, the members, and God! And no one

Healing the Shattered Soul

knew! We challenge churches everywhere to take heed of this Scripture. When you come together as a group, restrict your speaking in tongues as the Scripture directs. If you do so, you will have taken a major step in restricting Satan's attack on you. Three other Scriptures most churches overlook are:

"Beloved, believe not every spirit, but try the spirits whether they are of God: because many false prophets are gone out into the world. Hereby know ye the Spirit of God: Every spirit that confesseth that Jesus Christ is come in the flesh is of God: And every spirit that confesseth not that Jesus Christ is come in the flesh is not of God: and this is that spirit of antichrist, whereof ye have heard that it should come; and even now already is it in the world." 1 John 4: 1-3

"And he said, take heed that ye be not deceived: for many shall come in my name ..." Luke 21:8

"Not everyone that saith unto me, Lord, Lord, shall enter into the kingdom of heaven; but he that doeth the will of my Father which is in heaven. Many will say to me in that day, Lord, Lord, have we not prophesied in thy name? And in thy name have cast out devils? And in thy name done many wonderful works? And then will I profess unto them, I never knew you: depart from me, ye that work iniquity." Matthew 7:21-23

This seems to be one of the areas of greatest confusion amongst Christians. Satanists can and do use the name of Jesus. They can teach and preach about in Luke and Matthew clearly show this. The one thing they can't do is pass the test given in 1 John 4. They cannot look you square in the eye and say, "Jesus Christ who is God, who came in the flesh, died on the cross and three days later arose from the grave and now sits at the right hand of God the Father, this Jesus is my Lord and Savior and Master.' Oh, they can say "Jesus saved me." But which Jesus are they talking about? Jesus Himself said that many would come claiming to be Him. They can also read or repeat a confession or profession of faith in Jesus Christ. They can and do read the Scriptures. If you ask them if Jesus Christ who came in the flesh is their Savior, they can lie and say "Yes." But they cannot, with their own mouth, make the declaration as given above. God gave us a test to use, dear brothers and sisters in Christ. Let us use God's word.

I can verify this testimony from other sources. I have ministered to several former satanists who give similar accounts. Elaine's testimony is the clearest summary of one troubling aspect of satanic practice as others have shared it with me.

Pastor and author Mark Bubeck records a time in his own life when speaking in tongues had become an issue. Mark experienced a false tongue and was able both to test and to eject the false spirit. The result was that he was able to enjoy a true spiritual tongue after expelling the false spirit.

"A problem arose in my life, however, when I began to find myself seeking such an experience as an evidence of God's special anointing. I can recall one such occasion when the results after the feelings had been there were discouraging indeed. The message had been delivered with great difficulty and a complete lack of liberty. I began to ask the Lord why. It was revealed through meditating on the Word that I was beginning to function on feeling and experience rather than upon fact and faith. I was impressed to see that when Satan draws near, the emotional and feeling responses of the body can be very similar to what had been experienced in the Holy Spirit's presence. Eliphaz, Job's friend, testifies to this fact in Job 4:15 when he states, "Then a spirit passed before my face; the hair of my flesh stood up" (KJV). The first time I read those words after the experience just related, I saw how my experience was similar to that of Eliphaz. The supernatural presence of any powerful spirit being can and often does precipitate some unusual body and soul feelings and sensations in us mortals. Those who have attended séances and other spiritualist meetings testify to such fact. The point of this observation is to emphasize strongly that we must not depend upon feeling and experience as an evidence of our being filled with the Holy Spirit.

"Even the so-called experience of speaking in tongues must be exercised with much care. Whenever anyone tells me that he speaks in an unknown tongue and that this is an evidence of the fact that he has been filled with the Spirit, as kindly as I can I ask him if he has tested the spirit? The Holy Spirit tells us to do this in 1 John 4:1-4. He will not be insulted by such a test. If you speak in an unknown tongue, I urge you to obey this instruction of the Spirit. While using a tongue, your own mind must be largely inactive. In your mind you can command the spirit behind the tongue to answer clearly with an answer to your mind, "Has Jesus Christ come in the flesh? Is Jesus Christ Lord?" Insist upon a clear definite affirmative yes. The Holy Spirit will always respond with a praising yes. Another spirit may well respond with some evasive answer or even a very blunt no. I know of cases where such testing has revealed the invasion of a wicked spirit into the experience of believers."[43]

Two important things to note from Bubeck's testimony are:

(1) **Do not let emotions be the "test of the spirit."** People may feel a sense of peace or elation after speaking in false tongues. Mormons use a "burning in the bosom" to be the definitive test of "truth." The enemy can give feelings of peace.

(2) **Just because a person has a false spiritual gifting does not mean that once the enemy is evicted he or she will not have a true gifting.** When a person has experienced a false gifting I try to encourage them with the prospect that God will still use them. Often these people are so hurt to learn that they have been deceived and may in fact have deceived others that they are very ashamed and could possibly quench their spirit for valid ministry.

Anita came to me from a charismatic church. When she would pray in her tongue her emotions would become so enraged that she would actually attack her brother physically. He was the pastor of a mid-sized church in Los Angeles. It was obvious to everyone in their church that Anita had a false tongue.

Anita brought her sister-in-law (the pastor's wife) as a prayer partner. (I always encourage people to bring Christian prayer partners with them to sessions.) We were able to isolate the spirit very quickly, but when it came to casting him out I encountered a difficulty. Apparently one of the beliefs in their church was that "tongue speaking" was a sign of salvation. If you could not speak in a tongue you were not saved. We could get rid of the spirit, but Anita simply could not speak in tongues without the enemy. Her chant to start her tongue was actually an invocation for calling in the enemy.

In Anita's case, I was more confident of her salvation than she was. She gave me a clear testimony that "Jesus saved her from her sin….." Judging from her presentation I would suspect that most congregants in her brother's church would also give a clear confession. Her sister-in-law tried to argue the theology with me, but she could see the evidence right in front of her face in the form of Anita. She had a choice: either Anita was not a Christian or her theology about tongues being a requirement for salvation was in question. Despite her arguments, I reminded Anita's sister-in-law that I did not do anything but remove a demon that had cussed at us when it was directed to say "Jesus came in the flesh." I had taught no theology. Anita and her sister-in law left troubled because they had a severe paradigm shift to make in the next few days.

Another example of false tongues is "The Way International," an organization or "church" where all congregants are encouraged to experience the "gift of tongues." According to the testimonies of its members, in fact, having the gift of tongues is practically equated with one's salvation. They speak about Jesus and teach that He is the way, yet the title of a book that the sect's founder penned is *Jesus Christ is Not God.*

Testing Memories

When a person has suffered from childhood abuse, sometimes memories have been encapsulated in the sub-personalities. Unfortunately, not all of these memories are true. Many parts have demonic spirits who have gained a foothold within the fortress walls. When this has occurred the spirits can twist the memories. Demons are liars and distorters whose main function is to steal, kill, and destroy. They can complete this mission through lies and distorted memories. They try to get us to see that the enemy is in the flesh, in our family members and trusted friends, and pit us against one another.

We see this in the Gospels with Judas and Jesus and even Peter and Jesus. In the Old Testament Saul was enraged at David through the assistance of an evil spirit. The spirit had convinced Saul that David was going to usurp his kingdom. This became such a stronghold in Saul's life that he became obsessed with David's destruction.

In ministry I encounter soul-pockets with divisive memories that accuse other family members of abuse. If the abuse is unknown and the family is unaware of the abuse, I immediately call in the head demon of highest authority to verify the memory, binding him to truth in Jesus' name. In most cases, I can find out immediately if the account is true, distorted, or a flat-out lie. Jesus really steps in at this point and holds demons accountable. This response is usually immediate, and the person senses that it is the real truth.

People sometimes come to me with "body memories." They have been taught that their body remembers the abuse or trauma they experienced and they need to be healed of these. In the past I have not challenged this notion of body memories. I have noticed, however, that after inner healing is complete and the demonic spirits are addressed a demon will invariably take credit for the affliction. In the last few years I address a spirit in charge of "body memories" if I suspect that one may be present. I break its strongholds and cut off any future assignment.

Chapter 2: Tracy's Story-The Deliverance Path

A Typical Counseling Session with Tracy

A demon speaks through Tracy: I don't believe that I can be fixed. Will God really give me someone? Will my loneliness finally end? I don't want to live any more. If my life consists of these emotions and this isolation, it is better that I am gone. My sister and others seem to have someone to love, to invest in, children to rear, a family to grow old with. Other women have someone to watch over them, a man who wants to protect and provide for them. I do not. I am a loser and have always felt that my friends, certain people, and married women see me as defective. I feel that I get appeased by them or receive a token comment but that I am by-passed because I don't matter. I am broken, they know it, and they want nothing to do with me.

Jim: Tracy, those are lies. You are a princess in God's kingdom. He loves you and is not going to abandon you. I believe a part or parts are beginning to surface through these feelings. A demonic spirit is enhancing your emotions. This is why it is so torturing. So what we need to do is invite them to accept Jesus and fuse them into the core so they aren't alone.

Tracy: No, this is what I really feel. Saying those words does not change anything. That makes me mad.

Jim: Tracy, every time we get here you make these statements, and every time when the part is healed and the enemy is removed you feel much better.

Jim Prays: Father, we pray against that head demon of highest authority over Tracy along with his entire network and gatekeepers that they would be bound, gagged, and rendered inoperative. The entire network is set aside in the name of the Lord Jesus Christ, the One who came in the flesh. Father, I speak past Tracy to that little child inside. You have been carrying a burden that little children should not carry. Would you like to come forward and talk about it?

Tracy: I feel so very alone and isolated from life. I feel like giving up. I have no one to love me. There will be no one—no matter what I do.

Jim: I bind the spirit of alone, isolation, and abandonment. I set you aside gagged and rendered inoperative.

Tracy: My parents weren't there for me. Something happened when I was so young and I don't know what. All I know is that I think I was abandoned cause Mom wasn't there. My dad was so mean and scary. Mom would retreat.

[Jim pauses as Tracy and her parts cry for about five minutes.]

Jim: The hollowness that you feel is because the Holy Spirit is not in you. He is the only One who can fill that emptiness. God loves you. He has had His eye on you from the very beginning. He wants you whole and healthy. He assigned angels over you from the very beginning because He knows you are His princess. But I want you to know that accepting Jesus is the path to begin your healing.

Tracy: Who is Jesus?

Jim: [I recognize that I am talking to a little girl who has never surfaced so I share the Gospel as I would with a child.] Jesus is God who created you and all of us. But we all rebelled against God and left Him through our bad things (sin). But He loves you so much that He wants you back in His family. So He came to earth to pay for our bad acts and died for them. He rose again demonstrating that He was successful. Now He offers to you the opportunity to come back into His family just by believing in Him and that He died for you. You must confess this with your mouth and believe it in your heart.

Tracy: How does that take away my pain?

Jim: God will seal you with His Holy Spirit, which will give you access to new emotions. He will give you love, joy, peace... . You can then give your burdens and pain to Jesus Christ. Jesus not only went to the cross to die for our sins but also to carry our emotional burdens. He bore our griefs and sorrows as well. The pain will go away when you integrate with the core and get behind the full armor of God so that the enemy won't be able to penetrate into your heart any more.

Tracy: I don't trust Him because He will draw me in and then abandon me. Everyone has abandoned me.

Jim: [I recognize these as stronghold lies.] I bind an enemy of doubt in Jesus' name and set you aside. Jesus will not forsake you. He will not leave you. When He seals you He will be with you through eternity. People will *sometimes* fail you—but not *always*. But Jesus will *never* fail you. Are you willing to accept Jesus as your Lord and Savior?

Tracy: I don't trust Jesus, and I am not sure this will work…but I am willing to try.

Jim and Tracy: [I lead the sub-part to confess that "Jesus came in the flesh" to distinguish it from demon imposters.] Repeat after me: I believe that Jesus is the Christ. He came in the flesh, died for my sins, and I now accept Jesus as my Lord, God, and Savior.

Jim: We now need to forgive those who have hurt you. Who do you need to forgive?

Tracy: I need to forgive my parents because they were not there for me. They abandoned me.

Jim and Tracy: [I lead the sub-part to forgive all people whom the part believes it needs to forgive. With a young child part I can typically go straight to the forgiveness, especially if it is a mother and father. With older parts I may have to teach on forgiveness, focusing on the principles in the chapter on forgiveness. I have her repeat it three or four times until one of us senses a release.] Repeat after me: I choose to forgive my mom in Jesus' name. I choose to forgive my dad in Jesus' name. I release them, let them go, and give them to Jesus.

Tracy: I still feel the pain.

Jim and Tracy: [At this point I have Tracy repeat out loud God's truths that address her injuries to appropriate the Word and its power to tear down the strongholds.] Repeat after me: I give the pain, the hurt, the grief, the sorrow to Jesus. He will not abandon me. He will be with me. He will love me and finish what He started. I am not alone, but I am part of the family of Christ. I am the bride of Christ, and He loves me with an everlasting love.

Jim: Are you ready to go into the core?

Tracy: Will I disappear?

Jim: No, you will just become a part of the whole. Imagine yourself as a pot of clay that has a piece broken off. We are just taking that piece that represents you and pressing it back into the whole. You don't disappear: You go back to where God wanted you in the first place.

Tracy: Can't I just stay separate?

Jim: God did not give two sets of armor. So it is important for you to be in the core where you can armor up and have protection against the enemy. This is how we will defeat the emotions, the hurts, the pains, and the sorrows. Those are the fiery darts that the enemy is sending your way. God says that a divided house will not stand. If you fuse into the core you will be able to stand and fight.

Tracy: Okay.

Jim: Can I talk to the core again?

Tracy: Yes, I am here.

Jim: Are you willing for this little girl to become one with you?

Tracy: Yes.

Jim prays: Based on your permission, I now pray. Father, will You put Tracy back to the way You envisioned her from before time began? I pray that she would become the woman that You designed. Lord, let her be in unity as You are in unity. I pray all this in Jesus' name.

[Tracy looks up, and I ask her if she felt anything. The person will typically experience some sensation. Her emotions always return to normal range.]

Tracy: I felt my heart move and the heavy emotions are almost gone.

[We might go through these prayers for each sub-part (which, in Tracy's case, is usually just two or three). Once the last part has been fused I go after the demonic spirits.]

Jim: Tracy, are you ready? Close your eyes. Head demon of highest authority, I command you front and center. Are you there?

Tracy: [Tracy will allow the demon to speak through her. Her body will physically arch and she will grin in a mocking way.] Yes, what do you want?

Jim: Do you have any legal rights?

Tracy: No.

Jim: [Apparently the enemy has no legal rights.] What are your strongholds?

Tracy: I don't need them. She will always be mine. She believes me—not you.

Jim: [From this statement I see two strongholds that need to be broken: (1) that the enemy owns Tracy and (2) that the enemy is the one to whom she should listen.] She is not yours. Jesus bought her. She is not even her own, but she is certainly not yours. She believes Jesus.

He is the One who is trustworthy, and she believes me to the extent that I follow Him.

Jim: [Jim continues to search for other strongholds and breaks them if necessary. Jim then has the demonic spirit remove any curses.] Head demon, repeat after me: I now remove every curse that I have placed upon Tracy, in Jesus' name. Are you ready to leave?

Jim and Tracy: I command you to leave and go to the foot of Jesus, in Jesus' name.

Tracy: I feel the release.

Jim: How do you now feel about Mom and Dad?

Tracy: It is strange. I feel totally different. All of the sudden I can remember the good things about my parents. Just a few minutes ago my emotions were so different. I love my parents.

Jim: What Tracy experienced here is very common. Once the dissociation is resolved and the enemy is removed, past hurts seem to disappear.

Reflections on the Journey

Tracy: Each person will have different experiences with the way in which sub-parts affect their emotions and surface into the conscious level. For instance, for some people the parts will surface but the person's core will remain engaged and so there may be an inner dialogue between the core and the sub-part. For me, when the sub-part surfaces I become the part. The enemy becomes my emotions. I experience the full array of the enemy's thoughts and feelings designed to get me just to give up. Until I get the part fused into the core I am unable to do much warfare.

Demonization accompanies the gay lifestyle. Entering into a same-sex relationship opens the door to the enemy by creating a legal right that allows demonic spirits to influence a person's sexual preference, sexual drive, and sexual attraction. The demon heightens sexual preoccupation.

When I was in the gay lifestyle I had ancestral spirits, an incubus spirit (a masculine enemy), and a succubus spirit (a feminine enemy) that drove me toward women and away from men. Satan's goal is to defile God's creation, and so he reverses how people feel internally toward themselves and members of the same sex and even provokes a disdain for members of the opposite sex.

I had sought healing for many years and wondered if I was sentenced to living in ambivalence the rest of my life, which meant that

I would be alone. Although I never contemplated suicide, the enemy's ultimate goal was that I take my life. The enemy comes to steal, kill, and destroy. I have known people personally in the gay lifestyle who have ended their life. The decision to end their life may not even have had to do with homosexuality at all, yet their lifestyle opened the door to the enemy, who then had opportunity to wreak havoc in their lives. Same-sex relationships enable the enemy to have a legal right, and once a demon has the right to influence a person's life it will seize every opportunity to ruin it in as many ways as possible.

The succubus spirits that afflicted me are generational and quite strong in my extended family. They have come down through my parent's generation and several family members practice the gay lifestyle. The succubus spirit expressed itself through my struggles with same-sex attraction, but it was also active in my relationships with family members.

When I arrived at Moriah Ministry, I was in a same-sex relationship that was a connection I could not break even with the help of a therapist. I knew that God wanted me to make changes, and I could not let go of the words He spoke to me. Every time I tried to separate from that relationship, however, the sub-parts would emerge and I would end up on the floor sobbing and incapacitated. I even lost jobs on occasion because the inner turmoil rendered me unable to cope.

Jim and I met weekly for almost six months discussing theology and issues about men. The sub-parts T2 and Clarissa finally had a voice with someone who wanted to listen and showed them love and they could express their fears. We prayed weekly, made contact with different sub-parts, confessed sins, and practiced forgiveness.

I remember the day that I was free from same-sex attraction and homosexuality. I actually felt that the child inside (Clarissa) had grown up (integrated) and that, at last, I was a woman. In fact I remember telling Jim: "I am a woman." Although we had spent time that week integrating T2 and Clarissa, I was amazed that I was free and felt so different. I knew that something drastic had happened. The Lord had done the miracle He said He would do.

Once T2 and Clarissa were integrated, I was able to end my same-sex relationship and a few weeks later, my counseling. I no longer felt so much like a child in court and was not as triggered by authority figures. Decision-making came much easier as I began to understand

and relate to my internal sub-parts. The power of the succubus system was broken!

I was able to read the Bible and attend church on a regular basis—both of which had been difficult for me. I found that making difficult and unpopular decisions became possible, including quitting my position as an associate to start my own practice. Most importantly, I was able to tell my long-time friends in the gay community that I was choosing a different lifestyle. They are still my friends.

Many Christians view those who are demonized as weak, not having a strong relationship with God, or unwilling to submit to the Lord's direction. This is a deception. Both Christians and non-Christians are demonized and yet remain oblivious to the fact that many of their physical and emotional problems stem from demonic attack. They end of up living under the oppression instead of recognizing the demonization and taking spiritual authority. In my instance, even though I recognized a spiritual oppression around me, I did not connect it with demonic spirits. I now understand that to a great extent the enemy controlled my emotions and self-beliefs, which in turn controlled my actions.

Jim: I had to show Tracy that there was hope and a future (Jeremiah 29:11). Each time we met we had to do inner healing and also address the enemy due to the strongholds in her life. As we progressed week after week in the process of inner healing, Tracy's core strength began to build. She was able to gain minor victories. As Tracy shared her story and the incremental victories that she achieved, I interpreted this as a sign that in the spiritual world the enemy was losing his footholds. His strength was diminishing, and Tracy's spirit was getting stronger.

Although at several points during the first six months Tracy enjoyed marked partial deliverance, we were unable to completely release her from the grip of the first strongman until we were about six months into the process.

One frustrating aspect of her deliverance was that the parts would only surface one at a time or, at the most, two at a time. It became something of a waiting game as events in her life would have to occur to trigger the "next" part. At the very least we would have to wait a couple of days after each healing.

On the positive side, each deliverance/healing occurred very quickly, sometimes with meetings less than 15 minutes. On rare occasions we could even do it over the phone. As Tracy became skilled at identifying when a sub-part surfaced, she was able to tell me what was going on inside so that we could heal the sub-part quickly. After a while, nearly all of Tracy's parts knew who Jesus was and how to pray to ask the Holy Spirit to enter into the part and integrate into the core.

One day I was finally able to get the strongman (the head demon of highest authority) to respond. From that day forward Tracy would enjoy freedom for extended periods of time, sometimes a whole week. Although at first it was very encouraging, in time Tracy became frustrated because it seemed as though it would never end. I knew she was getting discouraged, but I could also see victories in her daily life.

When I tried to send the head demon to the foot of Jesus he would go…but then he would always return some time later. It was as though he was hovering off in the distance only to affect her as a part surfaced. I have seen this in a few cases. It is as though God is allowing it to occur to ensure that we stay connected to Him and engaged in the process until the inner healing is complete.

In Tracy's case the head demon, which was a succubus, responded to her formal name on her birth certificate. Its goal was to defile Tracy sexually, and the means to do so was through inciting same-sex attraction. The flipside, associated with a spirit called "alone," was also empowered and working in conjunction with the succubus enemy. Even the succubus spirit, which was primarily a sexual enemy, was working to isolate Tracy and make her Tracy feel all alone.

Demonic spirits magnified the depression and worked in conjunction with the succubus spirit to keep Tracy linked with her same-sex partner. The enemy exercised power over Tracy's life through a defeating double bind: on the one hand she had a deep need for connection (maintained via the soul tie) to avoid her aloneness and on the other hand she knew that "it was wrong." God guides by subtle invitation, whereas the enemy accuses with deep guilt and shame. Those harsh accusations coupled with her inability to break from her partner were tearing Tracy apart internally.

Tracy would retreat to T2, who was tied to Clarissa. T2 was self-sufficient and unemotional. She took no guff and justified everything Tracy did. T2 could make it without anyone and was empowered by a spirit of pride that prevented her from experiencing any internal pain. This spirit drove her to the rebellious stage. If she could not fit in then she would be a total outcast.

As we progressed, I was able to detect whenever Tracy achieved a specific victory. We broke the power of T2 and Clarissa working together and integrated them on the same day. The primary stronghold for Clarissa was that she believed that she had to depend on human beings for her emotional strength. It was important for me to gain Clarissa's trust before we could really talk about Jesus and how *He* was the only One who could fill the hole in heart. Once I had gained her trust I was able to lead Clarissa to trust Jesus. Once we got her to shift her trust to Jesus to provide for her emotional needs it was quick work to get her in agreement to let go of her burdens and finally fuse into the core. With T2 it was a matter of convincing her that God could do a better job of protecting Clarissa than she could. The important truth for her to learn was that she had neither the ability nor the spiritual equipment to protect Clarissa from spiritual assault such as depression, rage, and being alone.

Once the succubus system was in retreat the secondary system shifted into power, headed by the spirit of "Alone" associated with Tracy's flipside. "Alone" kept Tracy from participating in life. Parts associated with Alone were the flipside, outcast, sad, devastation, despair, hopeless, and numerous small child parts created in the first three years of Tracy's life. Because it was difficult to get all the parts to surface this part of the process of Tracy's healing spanned several months. As each successive sub-part was healed and fused, Tracy's life changed for the better. Her spiritual life was strengthening with a commitment to minister. Her newfound confidence in her ability at work enabled her to make a personal decision to "go it alone" and start her own law practice.

Afterword: A Final Note of Encouragement

My purpose in writing this book was to give hope to those who are suffering from dissociation and to equip those who want to step into this ministry. My prayer is that many will be able to step into this ministry so that Christians can experience the freedom that Jesus promises. After 21 years of doing this ministry I am convinced that at least one person in every family suffers from dissociation. I do not believe that starting this healing ministry requires any special gifting. Rather, the gifting will come as the ministry is engaged.

Many find the prospect of beginning this ministry daunting. They feel overwhelmed because there is so much to know and understand regarding deliverance and inner healing. Take heart! The truth is that Jesus will walk with you, guide you, protect you, and fill in the gaps where you may fall short. When I was thrust into this ministry many years ago I was far less equipped than many of you reading this book, but God began to show me, to teach me, and to keep me from stumbling.

For those who are stepping out in this ministry I want you to adopt several points of protection:

1. Do not fear. You are in authority and performing God's will.

2. Be sure to pray the prayers of protection. Two important prayers I use are quoted in the healing path are included below. Memorize them.

"I bind up the head demon of highest authority [sometimes using the formal name on the person's birth certificate]. I bind up the entire network reporting to the head demon. I also bind the gatekeeper spirits and shut down their ability to allow spirits into or out of the system. All spirits addressed are now bound, gagged, and rendered inoperative."

"I forbid any acts of vengeance or violence against any of our families, friends, or churches, in Jesus' name."

3. I recommend that each person who ministers go through the first two pages of the *Steps to Victory* (moriahfreedommiinistry.com) on a regular basis. Do the declarations out loud so that any spiritual source knows what you believe. I personally use it as a tool for confession and protection on a weekly basis. If you discern spiritual attack, take a few minutes and read through the *Steps to Victory* immediately, focusing especially on the initial section **"Repentance from Idolatry."** Reading or declaring this section will cancel any prayer that dark sources have directed toward you.

Finally, understand that after accessing the parts (sub-personalities) the key things that you will be doing are evangelism, confession of sin, forgiveness, and declaring spiritual truth to shatter the enemy's strongholds. Christians are the only people who are equipped to do this kind of ministry. If we do not do it, it will not be done. Traditional counseling will address only symptoms whereas Christians have the tools to root out the cause.

Consider the following suggestions as you minister to those seeking freedom:

1. **Commitment:** I usually schedule two hours for my first session and 90 minutes for subsequent sessions. Most clients are healed in one or two sessions whereas others, like Tracy, have taken over a year.

2. **Attitude:** I approach every client with mercy and grace. I judge no one until they are set free and able to make decisions without demonic influence.

3. **Theology:** Study the list "Who I am in Christ" in the appendix to this book so that you will be able to knock down demonic strongholds. As you begin to understand those passages in scriptural context you will be able disarm the spirits.

James L. Hanley & C. Tracy Kayser

Glossary

Ancestral Demon: An ancestral demon is one that has come down through the family line due to a legal right gained in previous generations. If a sin is unconfessed a demon may have gained a right and stay in a person's life. Then it will pass down to the person's children and grandchildren when an opportunity arises. This does not mean that the inheriting person is guilty of the sin. But it may mean that the person is tempted in a like manner far more than another person who has no such ancestral enemy. The strongest ancestral demon will take on the formal name of the person as stated on his or her birth certificate. It will also be the head demon. Ancestral demons seem to be the strong enemies we encounter.

Demonization: I use the term demonization (as do many others in deliverance ministries) rather than the common translation "demon-possession." Demon-possession imputes too much power to the enemy and implies that the spirit owns the person. Instead the person is victimized (but not *owned*) by the enemy as suggested in parallel translations that are worded the person "had a demon." These translations more nearly reflect the actual person-demon relationship.

Dissociative Identity Disorder (DID): This term covers a whole range of symptoms from minor dissociations such as those that manifest in panic attacks or depression to major pathologies such as Multiple Personality Disorder (MPD). I think of it as a continuum of symptoms. The chapter on Dissociation helps to explain this condition further. Synonyms in this work include: Traumatic Memories (TM); Soul Pocket; Part, Sub-personality.

False memories: Memories are sometimes distorted by demonic influence. Demons are incredibly adept at distorting truth, even to the extent of replaying events in our past and reproducing scenes that were fabricated by the enemy. Therefore we should test all memories that affect family relationships coming from dissociative parts. I interrogate the spirit to find what he has done. Often they are proud to tell you all the nefarious schemes they have achieved.

Flipside: A flipside is created by an Ancestral Demon whose legal right is traced back in the family lineage. A flipside will act on the ancestral demon's behalf to sabotage a person's life. The flipside is created in the womb shortly after conception. The flipside will act like a multiple personality except that it will never come forward. Instead, it will control the person's life from behind the scenes. A person with a flipside will never be able to enjoy full Christian victory until the flipside is dealt with along with the ancestral spirit.

Head Demon: It appears that in the spiritual realm the enemy is organized in military ranks. Just as in military organizations there is a head leader usually called a "general" in human armies. The head demon is the one in charge. It will often be an ancestral spirit (see the definition above). Each demon will report to one over it in rank, just as in human military hierarchies.

Interject: An interject is similar to a dissociative identity with two differences. An interject is demonically created and contains no measure of faith. It will not accept Christ but can be removed by merely asking the Lord to remove it. An interject is typically distinguished by being an internal image (in voice and appearance) of a perpetrator in the person's life.

Power Encounter: A power encounter occurs whenever we directly address the enemy. It does not require yelling or screaming. The power is in Christ *not* in the level or intensity of our voice. When we do power encounters and address the enemy we are looking for two things: (1) the legal right (how the enemy got in) and (2) the stronghold (the lie that allows the enemy to stay in).

Strongholds and Fortresses: In this book I distinguish between strongholds and fortresses. In the illustration of the exodus and entrance into the Promised Land, a Dissociative Identity Disorder (DID) is analogous to the battle of Jericho, while the deception of the Gibeonites is analogous to a stronghold. A **stronghold** is a belief that is in opposition to a truth of God. A **fortress** is when a belief is so entrenched that a wall is created that causes part of the soul to separate into a pocket of operating as a dissociated identity. **Trigger:** A trigger is an event or spoken word(s) that will cause a sub-personality to begin to surface from the unconscious area of our soul. The alter will usually come to an emotional level, though sometimes it will surface all the way to a conscious level.

Truth Encounter: I distinguish between a truth encounter and power encounter as Charles Kraft does in *Defeating Dark Angels*. A *power encounter* is when we go into the garage and shoot the rats (demons). A *truth encounter* is when we go into the garage and clean it out. Taking someone through the steps to freedom would be an example of a truth encounter.

James L. Hanley & C. Tracy Kayser

Bibliography

Albright, Joe, *Liberating the Bruised* (Houston: Joe Albright Evangelistic Assn, 1967).

Allender, Dan B. *The Wounded Heart* (Colorado Springs: Navpress, 1990).

Amstutz, Wendell. *Exposing and Confronting Satan & Associates.* National Counseling Resource Center (Rochester, MN, 1992)

Anderson, Neil. *Victory over the Darkness* (Ventura, CA: Regal, 1990); *The Bondage Breaker* (Eugene, OR: Harvest House, 1990). *Helping Others Find Freedom in Christ* (Ventura , CA: Regal Books, 1995).

Basham, Don. *Can a Christian Have a Demon ?* (Monroeville, PA: Whitaker House, 1971); *Deliver Us From Evil* (Old Tappan, NJ: Revell, 1972, 1980).

Bernal, Dick. *Curses* (Shippensburg, PA: Companion Press, 1991).

Birch, George A. *The Deliverance Ministry* (Cathedral City, CA: Horizon, 1988).

Blue, Ken. *Authority to Heal* (Downers Grove, IL: InterVarsity, 1987).

Brown, Rebecca. *He came to set Captives Free* (Chino, CA: Chick Publishing, 1986).

Bubeck, Mark. *The Adversary* (Chicago, IL: Moody Press, 1975); *Overcoming the Adversary* (Chicago, IL: Moody Press, 1984); *The Satanic Revival* (San Bernardino, CA: Here's Life, 1991).

Dickason, C. Fred. *Demon Possession and the Christian* (Chicago, IL: Moody Press, 1987).

Friesen, James. *Uncovering the Mystery of MPD* (San Bernardino, CA: Here's Life, 1991).

Garrett, Susan R. *The Demise of the Devil* (Minneapolis, MN: Fortress, 1989).

Garrison, Mary. *How to Conduct Spiritual Warfare* (Hudson, FL: Box 3066, 1980).

Gibson, Noel and Phyllis. *Evicting Demonic Squatters and Breaking Bondages* (Drummoyne, NSW, Australia: Freedom in Christ Ministries, 1987).

Goodman, Felicitas D. *How about Demons?* (Bloomington, IN: Indiana Univ., 1988).

Green, Michael. *I Believe in Satan's Downfall* (Grand Rapids, MI: Eerdmans, 1981); *Exposing the Prince of Darkness* (Ann Arbor, MI: Servant, 1981).

Greenwald, Gary L. *Seductions Exposed* (Santa Ana, CA: Eagle's Nest Publications, 1988).

Groothuis, Douglas R. *Unmasking the New Age* (Downers Grove, IL: InterVarsity, 1986); *Confronting the New Age* (Downers Grove, IL: InterVarsity, 1988).

Hammond, Frank and Ida Mae. *Pigs in the Parlor* (Kirkwood, MO: Impact Books, 1973); *Demons & Deliverance in the Ministry of Jesus* (Plainview, TX: The Children's Bread Ministries, 1991).

Harper, Michael. *Spiritual Warfare* (Ann Arbor, MI: Servant, 1984).

Hughes, Robert Don. *Satan's Whispers: Breaking the Lies that Bind,* (Nashville, TN: Broadman Press, 1992).

Kallas, James. *Jesus and the Power of Satan* (Philadelphia , PA: Westminster, 1968).

Kinnaman, Gary D. *Overcoming the Dominion of Darkness* (Old Tappan, NJ: Revell,1990).

Koch, Kurt. *Between Christ and Satan* (Grand Rapids, MI: Kregel, 1962, 1971); *Occult Bondage and Deliverance* (Grand Rapids, MI: Kregel, 1970); *Demonology Past and Present* (Grand Rapids, MI: Kregel, 1973); *Occult ABC* (Grand Rapids, MI: Kregel, 1986).

Kraft, Charles H. *Christianity with Power* (Ann Arbor, MI: Servant, 1989); *Defeating Dark Angels* (Ann Arbor, MI: Servant, 1992); *Deep Wounds , Deep Healing* (Ann Arbor, MI: Servant, 1993)

Larson, Bob. *Satanism* (Nashville, TN: Nelson, 1989); *In the Name of Satan* (Nashville, TN: Thomas Nelson, 1996)

Linn, Dennis and Matthew. *Healing Life's Hurts* (New York, NY: Paulist Press, 1979); *Deliverance Prayer* (New York, NY: Paulist Press, 1981).

Lockwood, Craig, *Other Altars* (Minneapolis, MN: Compcare Publishers,1993).

Lutzer, Erwin W and DeVries, John F. *Satan's Evangelistic Strategy for this New Age* (Wheaton, Ill: Victor Books, 1989).

MacNutt, Francis and *Judith*. *Praying for Your Unborn Child* (New York, NY: Doubleday, 1988).

Mallone, George. *Arming for Spiritual Warfare* (Downers Grove, IL: Inter-Varsity, 1991).

Mayhue, Richard *Unmasking Satan* (Wheaton, Ill: Victor Books, 1988).

McAll, Kenneth. *Healing the Family Tree* (London: Sheldon Press, 1982).

Meyer. Joyce. *Battlefield of the Mind* (Tulsa, OK: Harrison House, 1995).

Montgomery, John W., ed. *Demon Possession* (Minneapolis, MN: Bethany, 1976).

Murphy, Ed. *Handbook for Spiritual Warfare* (Nashville, TN: Thomas Nelsen 1992).

Nevius, John R. *Demon Possession* (Grand Rapids, MI: Kregel, 1894, 1968).

Payne, Leanne. *The Healing Presence* (Wheaton, IL: Crossway,1989); *Healing Homosexuality* (Grand Rapids, MI, Baker Books, 1996).

Peck, M. Scott. *People of the Lie* (New York, NY: Simon & Schuster, 1983).

Penn-Lewis, Jessie. *War on the Saints* (9th ed). (New York, NY: Thomas E. Lowe, 1973).

Phillips, Ron. *Vanquishing the Enemy, Triumphant in the Battles of Life* (Cleveland, TN: Pathway Books, 1997).

Powell, Graham and Shirley. *Christian Set Yourself Free* (Westbridge. B.G.: Center Mountain Ministries, 1983).

Prince, Derek. *They Shall Expose Demons* (Grand Rapids, MI: Chosen Books, 1998).

Pullinger, Jackie. *Chasing the Dragon* (Ann Arbor, MI: Servant, 1980).

Reddin, Opal, ed. *Power Encounter* (Springfield, MO: Central Bible College, 1989).

Rockstad, Ernest. *Demon Activity and the Christian* (Andover, KS: Faith & Life Publications,1976).

Ryder, Daniel *Breaking the Circle of Satanic Ritual Abuse* (Miinneapolis, MN: CompCare Publisheers, 1992).

Seamands, David. *Healing for Damaged Emotions* (Wheaton, IL: Victor, 1981); *Putting Away Childish Things* (Wheaton, IL: Victor, 1982); *Healing of Memories* (Wheaton: Victor, 1985); *Healing Grace* (Wheaton, IL: 1988).

Savard, Liberty S. *Shattering Your Strongholds* (North Brunswik, NJ: Bridge-Logos Publishers, 1992).

Shaw, James D. and Tom C. McKenney. *The Deadly Deception* (Lafayette, LA: Huntington House, 1988).

Sherman, Dean. *Spiritual Warfare for Every Christian* (Seattle, WA: Frontline, 1990).

Shuster, Marguerite. *Power, Pathology, Paradox* (Grand Rapids, MI: Zondervan, 1987).

Subritzky, Bill. *Demons Defeated* (Chichester, England: Sovereign World, 1985).

Sumrall, Lester. *Demons: The Answer Book* (Nashville, TN: Nelson, 1987)

Tapscott, Betty. *Inner Healing through Healing of Memories* (Kingwood, TX: Hunter Publishing, 1975, 1987).

Unger, Merrill. *Biblical Demonology* (Chicago, IL: Scripture Press. 1952); *Demons in the World Today* (Wheaton, IL: Tyndale, 1971); *What Demons Can Do to Saints* (Chicago, IL: Moody Press, 1977).

Wagner, C. Peter. *Engaging the Enemy* (Ventura, CA: Regal, 1991).

Wagner, C. Peter and F. Douglas Pennoyer, eds. *Wrestling with Dark Angels* (Ventura, CA: Regal, 1990).

Warner, Timothy M. *Spiritual Warfare* (Wheaton, IL: Crossway, 1991).

White, Thomas B. *The Believer's Guide to Spiritual Warfare* (Ann Arbor, MI: Servant, 1990); *Breaking Strongholds* (Ann Arbor, MI: Servant, 1993)

Wimber, John. *Power Healing* (San Francisco, CA: Harper & Row, 1987).

Endnotes

[1] **Worsham, Roger** *Can a Christian be Demonized?* P4. Unpublished pamphlet.

[2] 1 John 4:1-3 (NAS): "Beloved, do not believe every spirit, but test the spirits to see whether they are from God; because many false prophets have gone out into the world. By this you know the Spirit of God: every spirit that confesses that Jesus Christ has come in the flesh is from ^{God}; and every spirit that does not confess Jesus is not from God; and this is the {spirit} of the antichrist, of which you have heard that it is coming, and now it is already in the world."

[3] John 10:10.

[4] Luke 8:27-31.

[5] If a person "has" a demon then a logical assumption follows: that the person has the responsibility to let go. This view also takes away much of the fears that people have in dealing with a demon. They see that they have an active role in keeping or rejecting the enemy's presence.

[6] In Matthew 12:24 Jesus is accused by the Pharisees of using the power of Beezelbul, the prince of demons.

[7] The KJV translates both phrases as "has a demon" even though the second word is the one traditionally translated demon-possessed.

[8] **Swindoll, Charles R.** *Satan... The Occult*, page 4.

[9] Examples include Matthew 4:24; 8:16, 28, 33; 9:32; 12:22 15:22, etc.

[10] See Pharaoh in Exodus or the Romans 2:21-26 for examples of God hardening hearts.

[11] *The Epistle of Ignatius to the Antiochians*, page 221.

[12] Cyprian, page 1206.

[13] We are commanded to be filled with the Spirit in Ephesians 5:18. Paul also tells us to not quench the Holy Spirit in 1 Thessalonians 5:19.

[14] Jesus' body was missing from the tomb. This seems to imply that his physical body was transformed. His ability to appear and disappear, ascend into heaven walk

through walls or even partake in eating shows a wide spectrum of physical abilities of Jesus' glorified body. He further shares that we will be like Him. It is our hope to be transformed in body and spirit.

[15] See 2 Cor 12: 6-10.

[16] Belial is an epithet for Satan or one of his generals. It was a name of a demonic spirit commonly known among the Corinthians.

[17] Taking drugs (not medication) is participating in mind-altering chemicals. This is "biblical" sorcery.

[18] Examples of this include Satan's request concerning Job (Job 1 and 2); Paul's thorn in the flesh (2 Cor 12:7); Saul's unclean spirit (1 Sam 18). This is the implication in Ephesians 4:26-27 where we are warned to not allow the sun go down on our anger lest the enemy gain a foothold in the believer's life. This is not to imply that all of God's discipline is through demonic spirits. God disciplines through many diverse methods.

[19] 1 Corinthians 15:36-58.

[20] Revelation 12 also describes Satan's obsession with the destruction of the saints.

[21] Job would be the classic example of this practice.

[22] Job 41:34 to end of book.

[23] Many expositors believe the man referred to in 2 Corinthians 7:12 is the same one that Paul turned over to Satan in 1 Corinthians 5:1-10.

[24] All mankind will be judged by either the Mosaic Law or the Law that man has created. See Roman's 2:12-14 for this teaching. (i.e. If I say, as a gentile, that people should not lie, I have created a law. I must then follow the law to the letter or I am guilty of sin.)

[25] Zech 14:10-11 All the land will be changed into a plain from Geba to Rimmon south of Jerusalem; but Jerusalem will rise and remain on its site from Benjamin's Gate as far as the place of the First Gate to the Corner Gate, and from the Tower of Hananel to the king's wine presses. 11 And people will live in it, and there will be no more curse, for Jerusalem will dwell in security.)

[26] Eph 4:26-27.

[27] **James Friesen** *Uncovering the Mystery of MPD* developed the concepts to a great degree in this book.

[28] **Kraft, Charles H.** *Deep Healing.* Dr Kraft outlines this in chapter 11 of *Deep Wounds.*

[29] **Kraft, Charles H.** *Deep Healing* . This is also Dr Kraft's understanding..

[30] **Amstutz, Wendell.** *Exposing and Confronting Satan & Associates* Pg 233=239.

[32] Paul discusses the struggle against his fleshly nature and how it had defeated him before Christ came into his life.

[33] 1 Corinthians 2:16

[34] I have been using a discovery first introduced to me by Dr. Joe Albright.

[35] In Isaiah 61 Jesus died for more than our sins, He also died for our Griefs and sorrows. By extension we can also say our abandonment or our traumas, because we know what happened to Him in going to the cross. In Hebrews 4 we are to be careful to grab onto every promise so that we can enter into His rest.

[36] **Albright, Joe,** *Liberating the Bruised.* 172-176.

[37] It also appears in James 4:8

[38] I refer to my sub-parts as distinct persons and do so because it seems easier to separate the sub-parts out from the core. However, I want to make clear that each sub-part is a part of the adult, a pocket of pain that had a distinct function, felt a specific age and yet was really the same age as the adult and a part of the adult.

[39] This can be found on our website at moriah-cell-church.com or in the near future at moriahfreedomministry.com.

[40] In dealing with demons I have relied heavily on Charles Kraft's *Defeating Dark Angels* and Joe *Albright's Liberating the Bruised.*

[41] **Anderson, Neil.** *The Bondage Breaker.*

[42] **Brown, Rebecca.** *He came to set Captives Free.* 235-237

[43] **Bubeck, Mark.** *The Adversary.* 40-42.

Acknowledgements

In the course of writing a book many individuals lent a helping hand to us. Charles Kraft (www.prayerministriesnetwork.com) who wrote the forward also added important insights throughout. He was at the beginning of this story and at the end. His help was invaluable. Another person that we owe a great debt is Scott Stewart. (www.ScottPhilipStewart.com) He probably edited every sentence in the manuscript except the few remaining where you might find errors. Finally, Gina Hanley, Pastor Jim's wife, spent many hours of editing and encouragement along the way.

Made in the USA
San Bernardino, CA
10 April 2016